PIANO / VOCAL / GUITAR

FOURTH EDITION

SONGS IN 3/4 TIME

ISBN 0-7935-0743-X

HAL•LEONARD® CORPORATION

7777 W. BLUEMOUND RD. P.O. BOX 13819 MILWAUKEE, WI 53213

Visit Hal Leonard Online at
www.halleonard.com

SONGS IN $\frac{3}{4}$ TIME

ALICE IN WONDERLAND

from Walt Disney's ALICE IN WONDERLAND

Words by BOB HILLIARD
Music by SAMMY FAIN

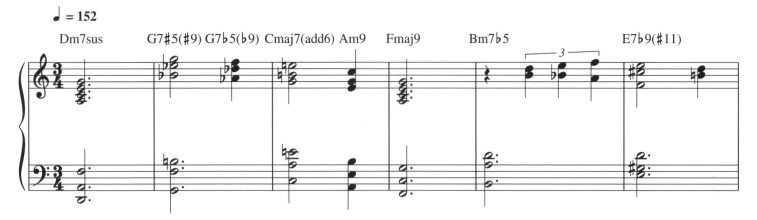

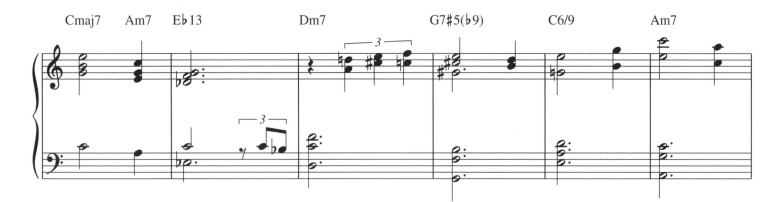

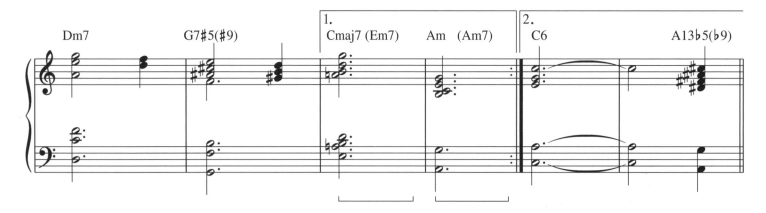

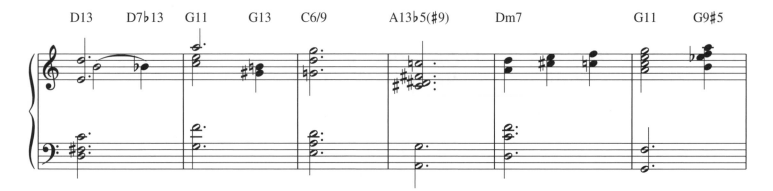

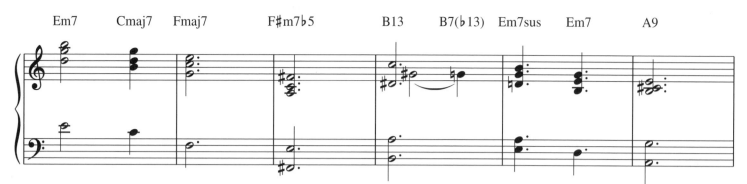

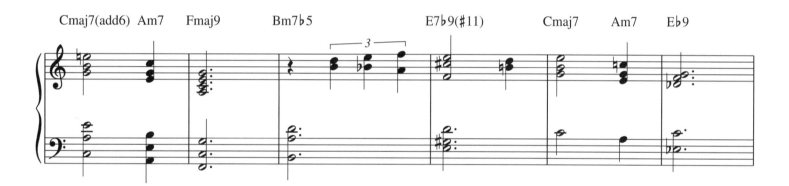

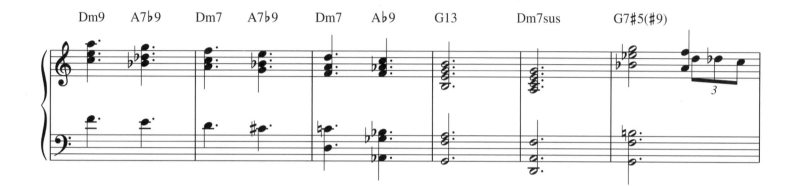

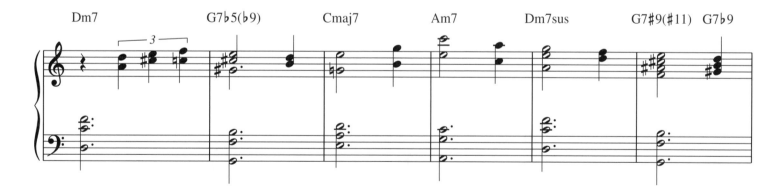

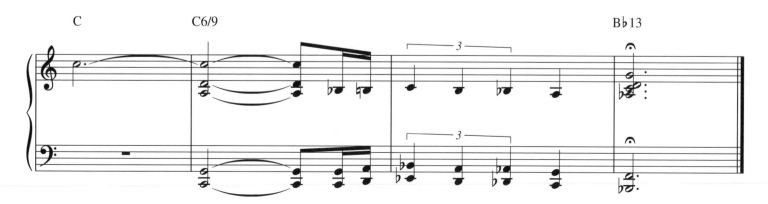

ALL ALONE

Words and Music by
IRVING BERLIN

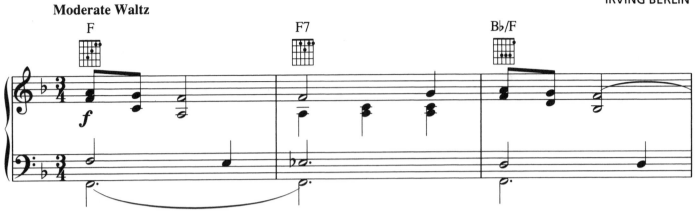

Just like a mel - o - dy that lin - gers on,
Just for a mo - ment you were mine,____ and then

ALLEGHENY MOON

Words and Music by DICK MANNING
and AL HOFFMAN

ALWAYS

Words and Music by
IRVING BERLIN

I'd for - get to smile. _____ Then I met
than the day be - fore, _____ till spring rolls

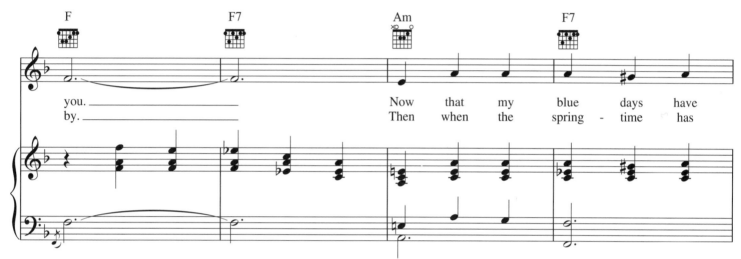

you. _____
by. _____

Now that my blue days have
Then when the spring - time has

passed, _____
gone, _____

now that I've found you at
then will my love lin - ger

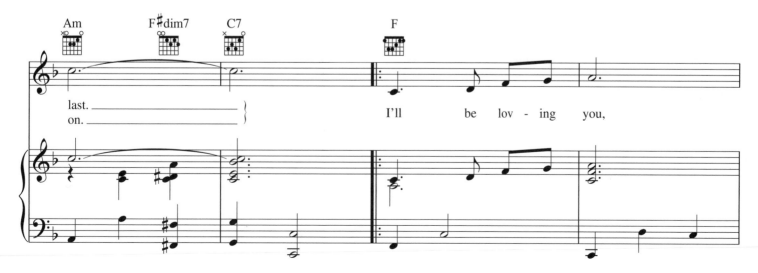

last. _____ }
on. _____ }

I'll be lov - ing you,

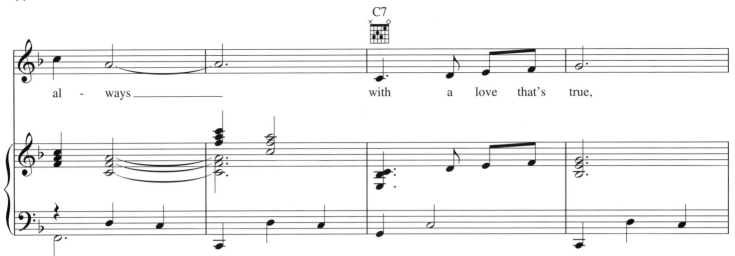

al - ways _____ with a love that's true,

al - ways. _____ When the things you've planned

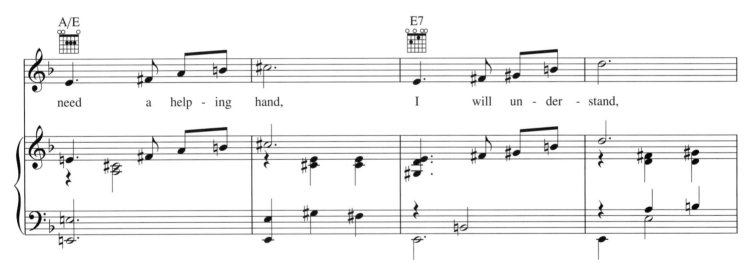

need a help - ing hand, I will un - der - stand,

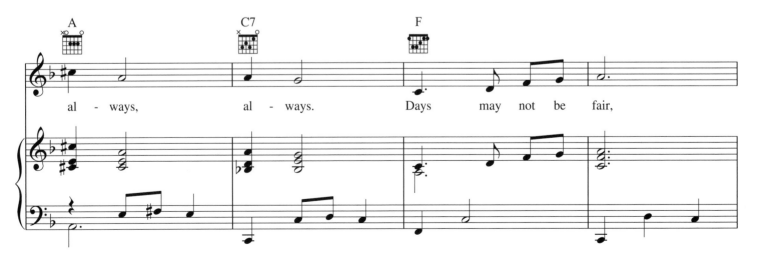

al - ways, al - ways. Days may not be fair,

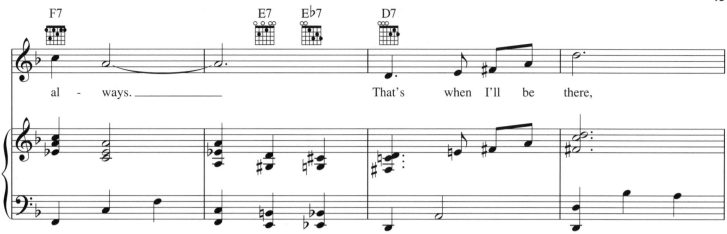

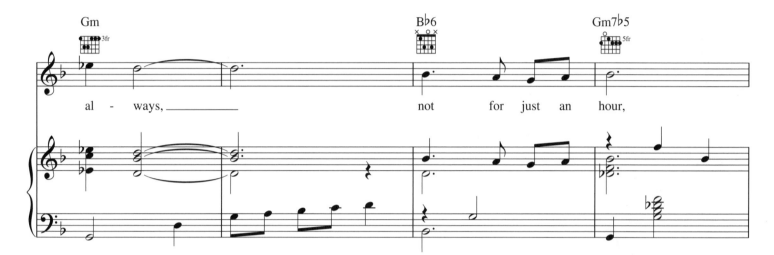

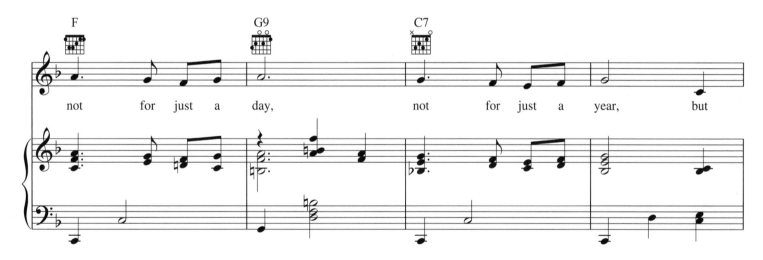

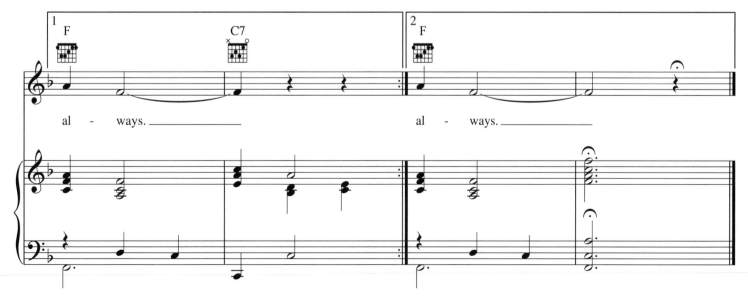

ANNIVERSARY SONG

from the Columbia Picture THE JOLSON STORY

By AL JOLSON
and SAUL CHAPLIN

Oh! how we danced on the night
night seemed to fade into blos-

we were wed. We vowed our true
-som-ing dawn. The sun shone a-

love though a word was-n't said.
new but the dance lin-gered on.

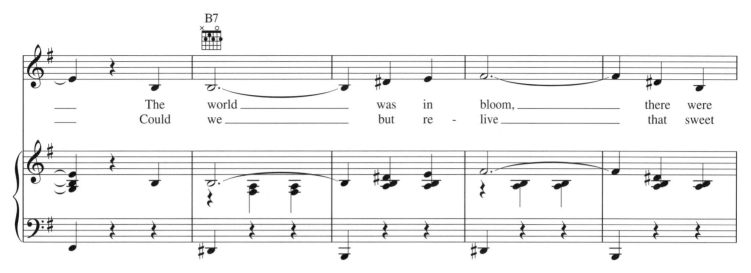

The world _____ was in bloom, _____ there were
Could we _____ but re - live _____ that sweet

stars _____ in the skies _____ ex - cept _____
mo - ment sub - lime, _____ we'd find _____

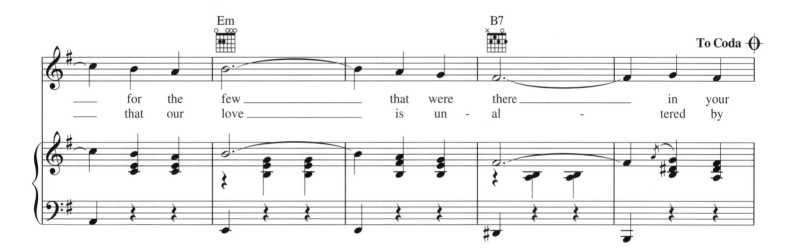

_____ for the few _____ that were there _____ in your
_____ that our love _____ is un - al - tered by

To Coda ⊕

eyes.

Dear, as I held you so

close in my arms, an - gels were sing - ing a

hymn to your charms. Two hearts gen - tly beat - ing were

mur - mur - ing low, "My dar - ling, I love you

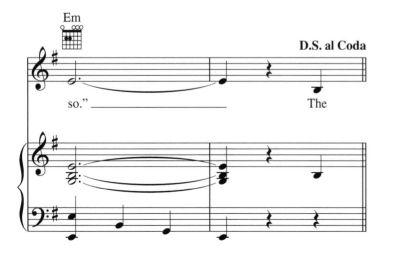

so." _____ The

time. _____

THE ANNIVERSARY WALTZ

Words and Music by AL DUBIN
and DAVE FRANKLIN

Moderate Waltz

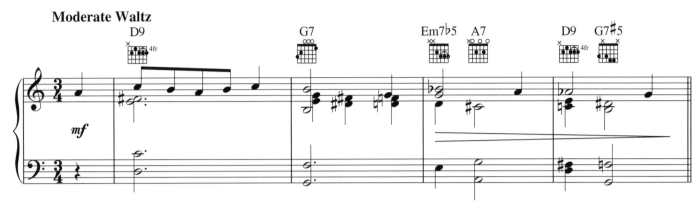

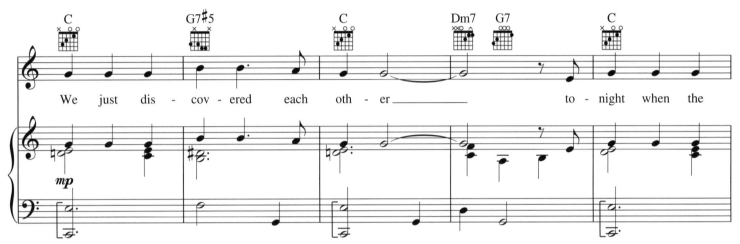

We just dis - cov - ered each oth - er _____ to - night when the

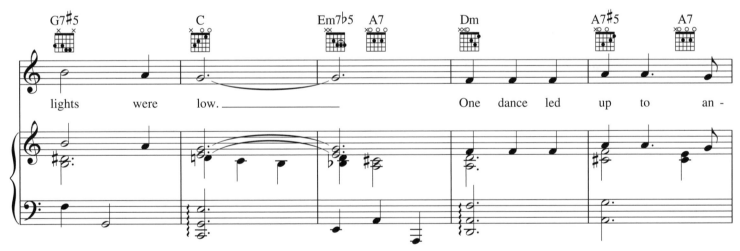

lights were low. _____ One dance led up to an -

oth - er, _____ and now I can't let you go, so:

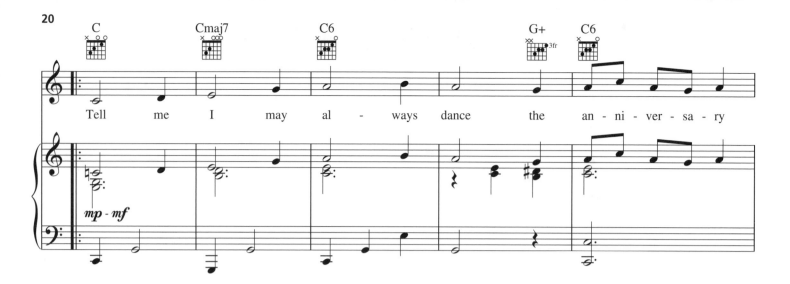

Tell me I may al - ways dance the an - ni - ver - sa - ry

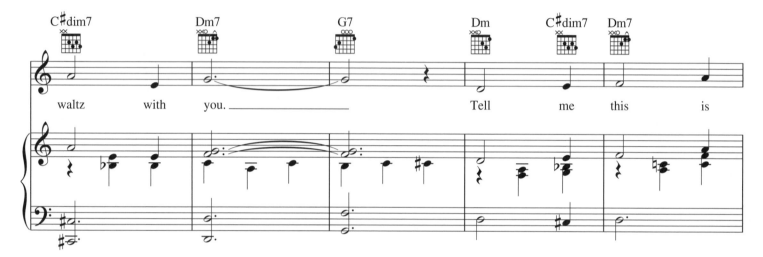

waltz with you. _____ Tell me this is

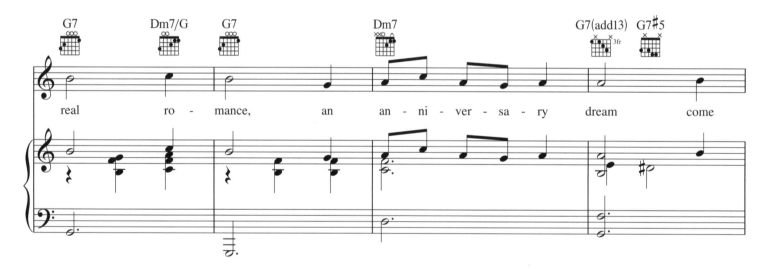

real ro - mance, an an - ni - ver - sa - ry dream come

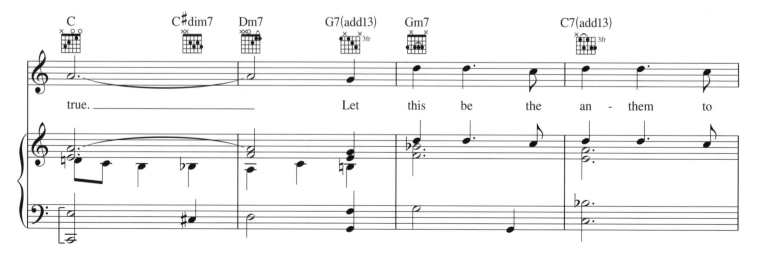

true. _____ Let this be the an - them to

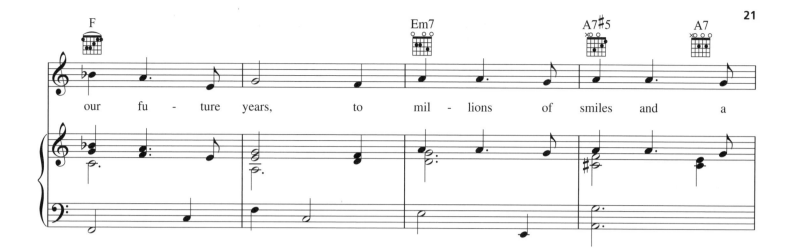

our fu - ture years, to mil - lions of smiles and a

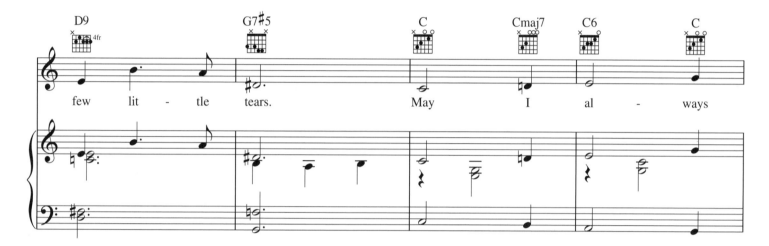

few lit - tle tears. May I al - ways

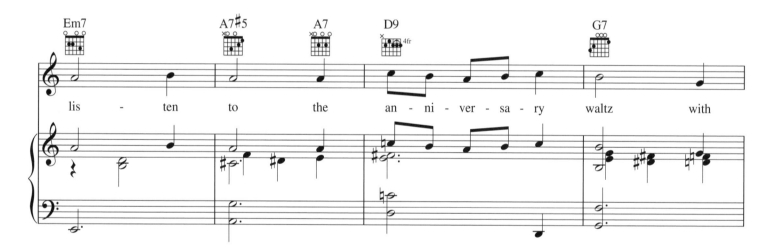

lis - ten to the an - ni - ver - sa - ry waltz with

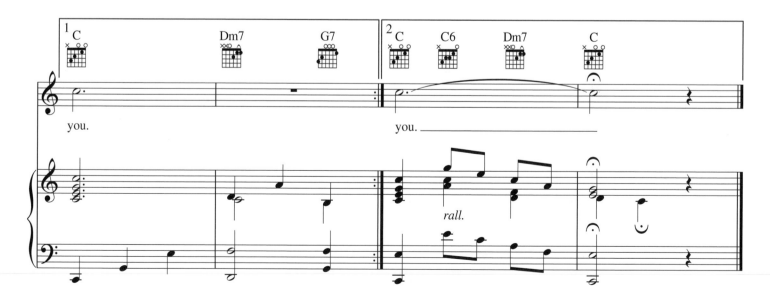

you.　　　　you. _____

rall.

AROUND THE WORLD

from AROUND THE WORLD IN EIGHTY DAYS

Words and Music by VICTOR YOUNG
and HAROLD ADAMSON

CAROLINA MOON

Lyric by BENNY DAVIS
Music by JOE BURKE

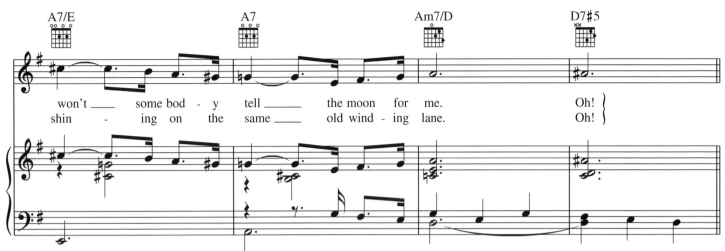

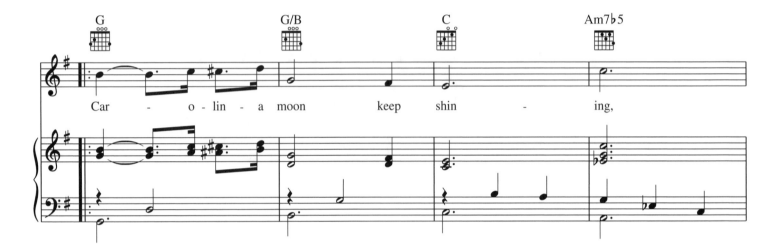

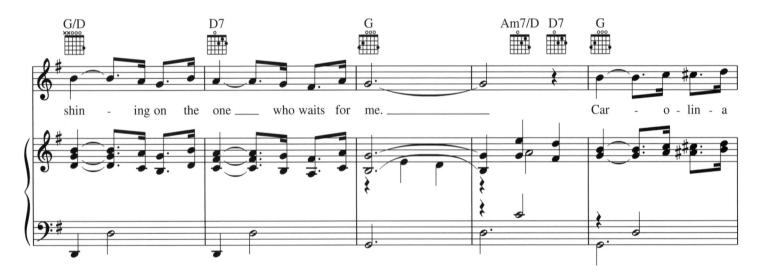

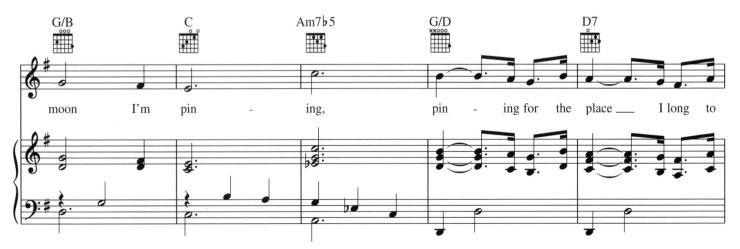

be. _____ How I'm hop-ing to-night you'll go, go to the right win-dow,

scat-ter your light, say I'm all right, please do. _____ Tell ___ her that I'm

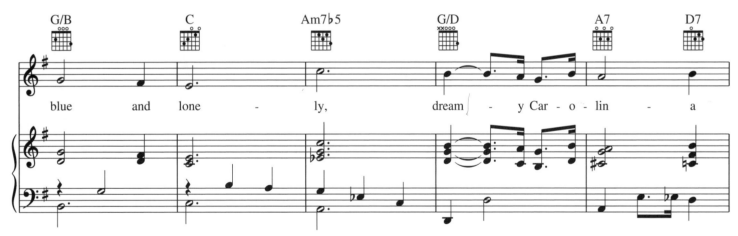

blue and lone - ly, dream - y Car - o - lin - a

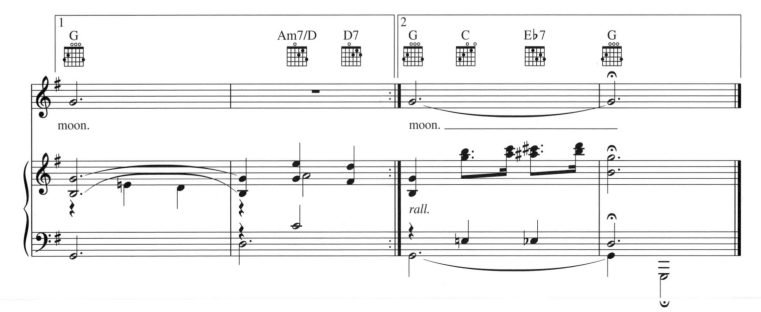

moon.   moon. _____

CARA, MIA

By JULIO TRAPANI and LEE LANGE

CHIM CHIM CHER-EE

from Walt Disney's MARY POPPINS

Words and Music by RICHARD M. SHERMAN
and ROBERT B. SHERMAN

DADDY'S LITTLE GIRL

Words and Music by BOBBY BURKE
and HORACE GERLACH

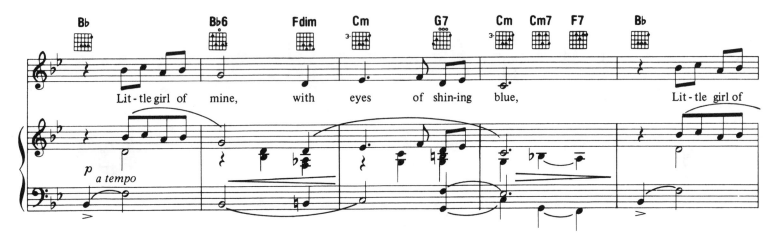

Lit-tle girl of mine, with eyes of shin-ing blue, Lit-tle girl of

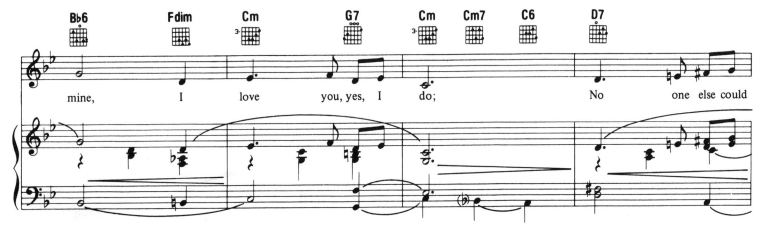

mine, I love you, yes, I do; No one else could

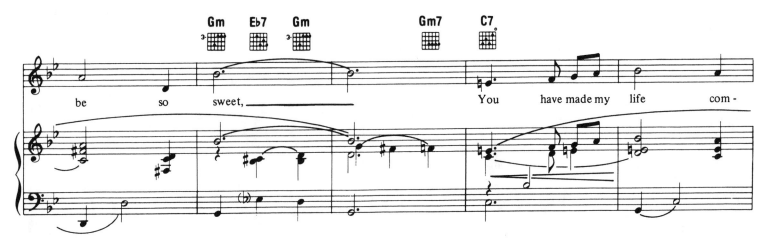

be so sweet, _____ You have made my life com-

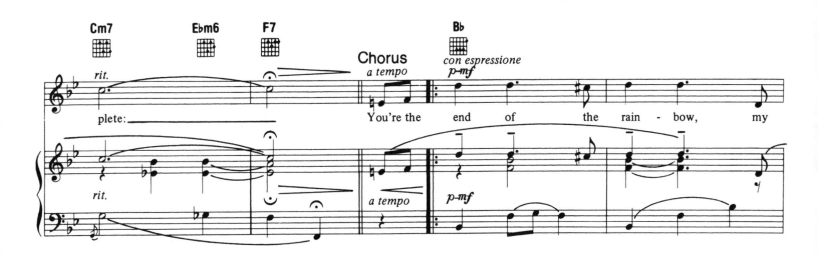

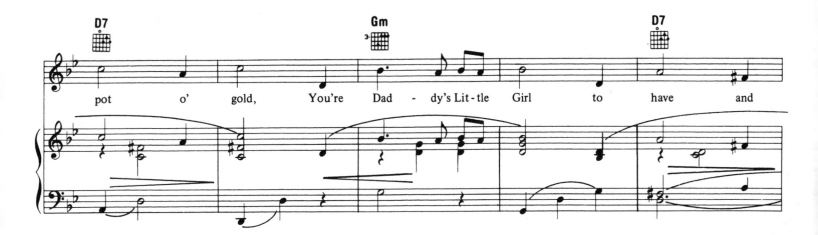

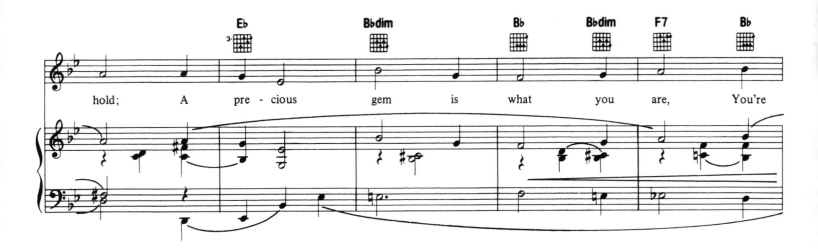

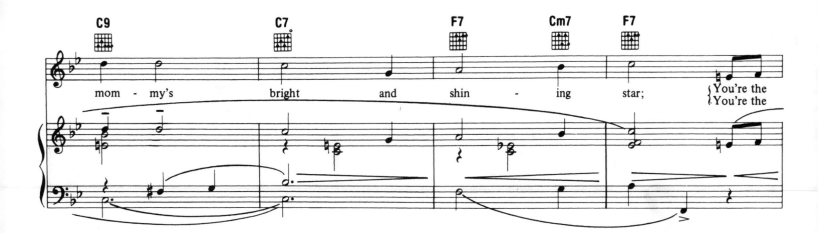

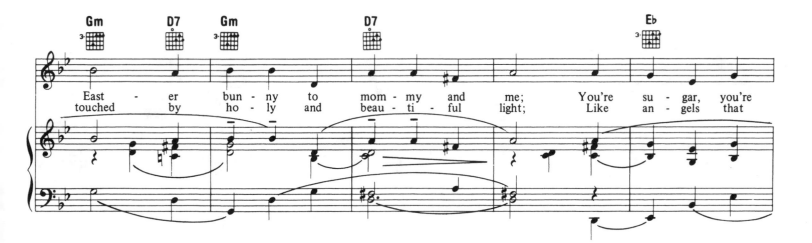

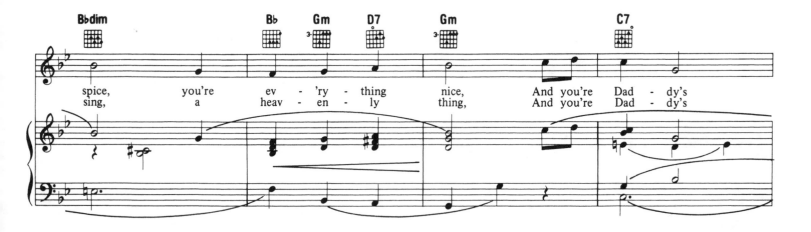

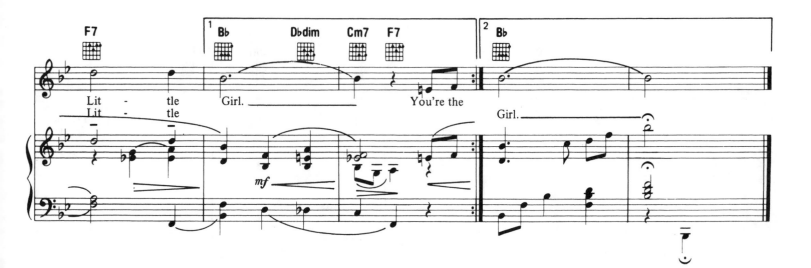

EDELWEISS
from THE SOUND OF MUSIC

Lyrics by OSCAR HAMMERSTEIN II
Music by RICHARD RODGERS

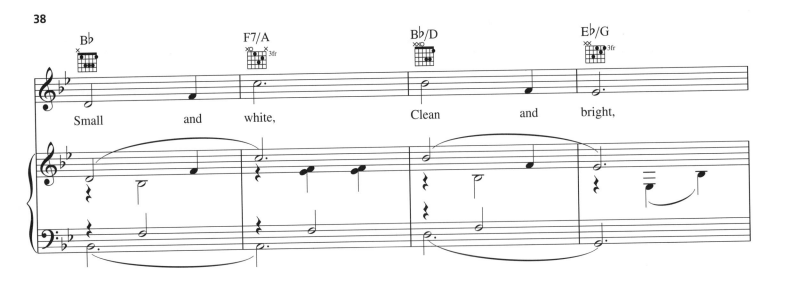

Small and white, Clean and bright,

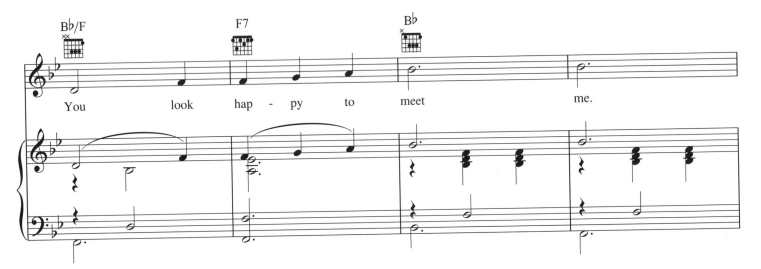

You look hap - py to meet me.

Blos - som of snow, may you bloom and grow,

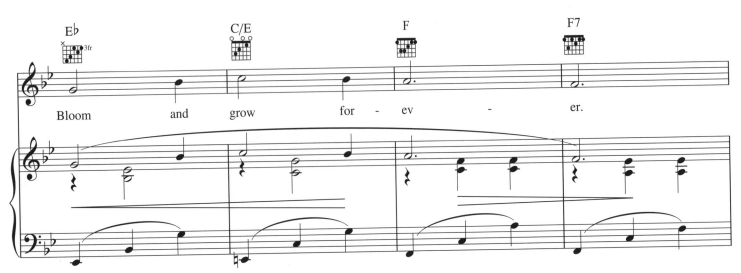

Bloom and grow for - ev - er.

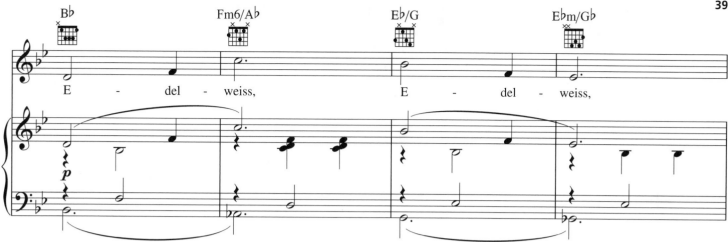

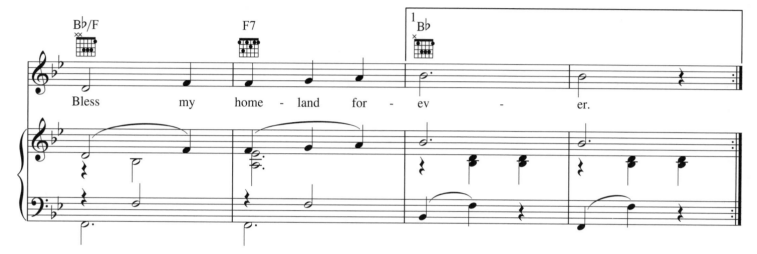

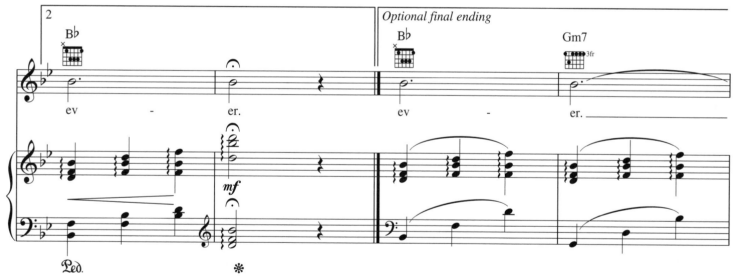

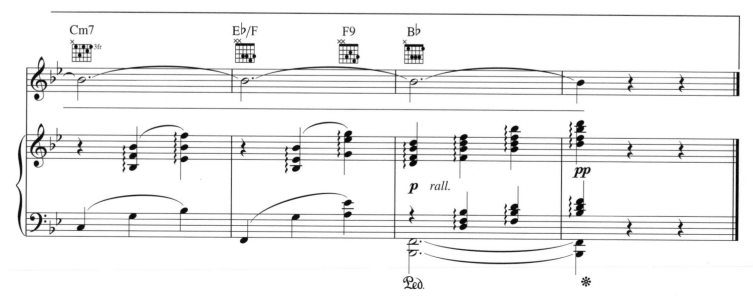

FALLING IN LOVE WITH LOVE
from THE BOYS FROM SYRACUSE

Words by LORENZ HART
Music by RICHARD RODGERS

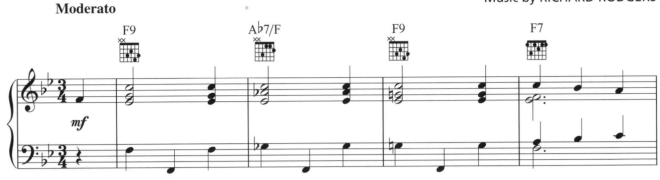

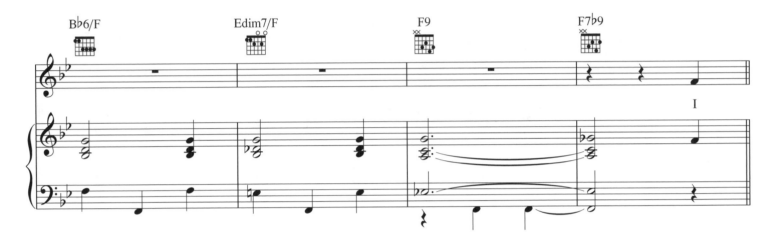

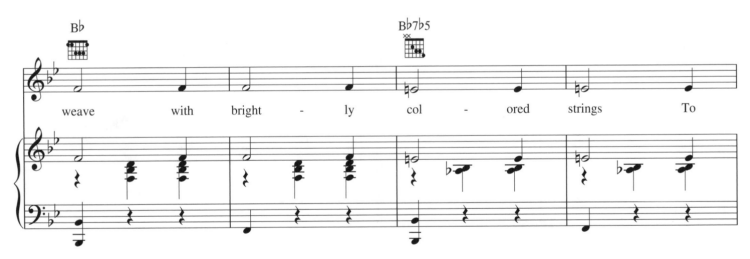

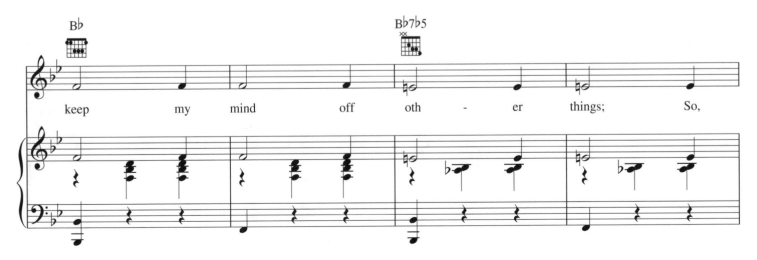

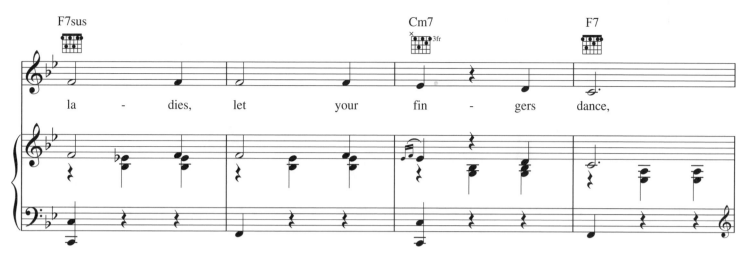

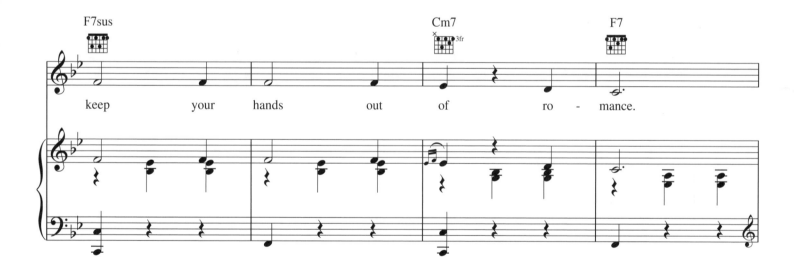

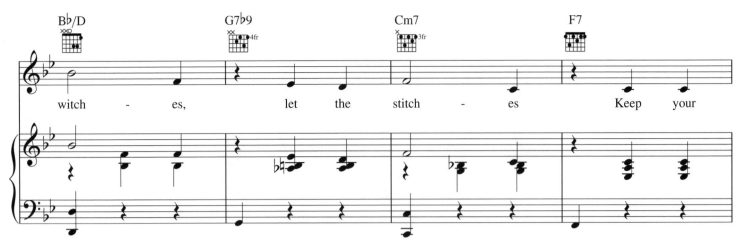

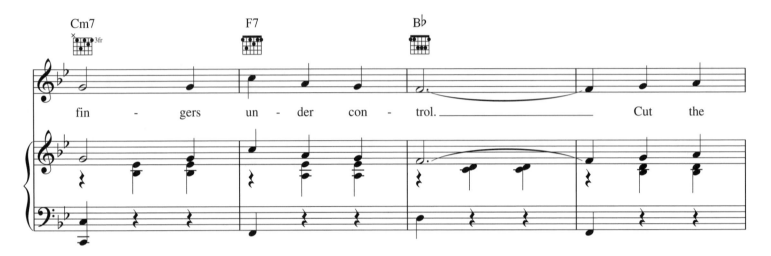

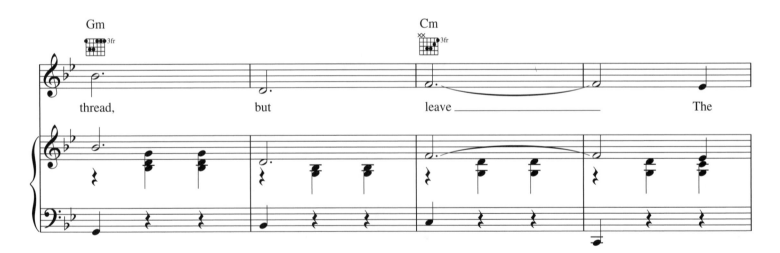

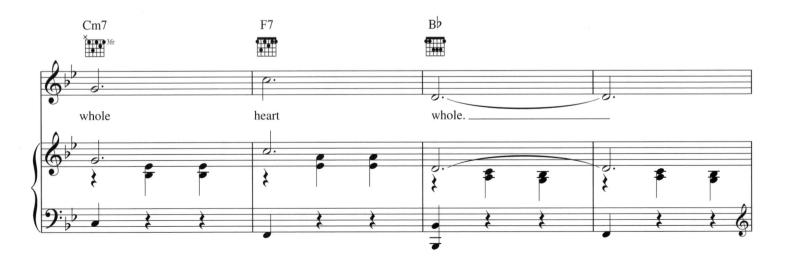

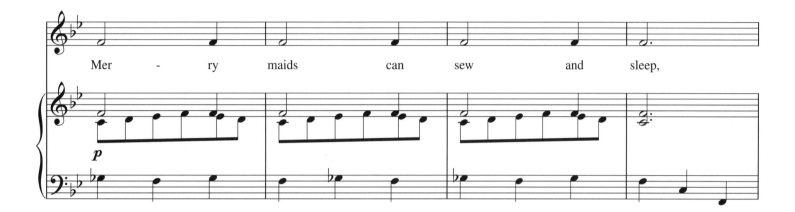

Mer - ry maids can sew and sleep,

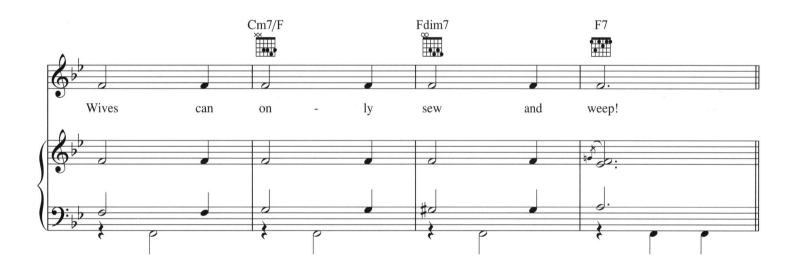

Wives can on - ly sew and weep!

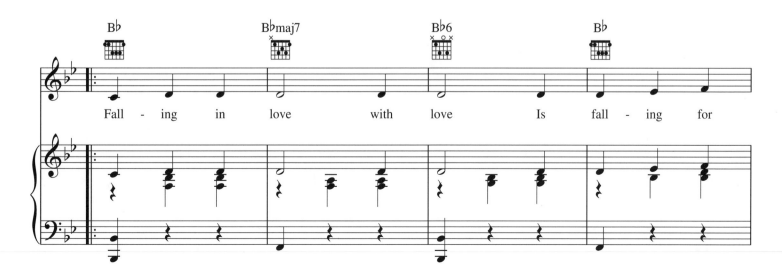

Fall - ing in love with love Is fall - ing for

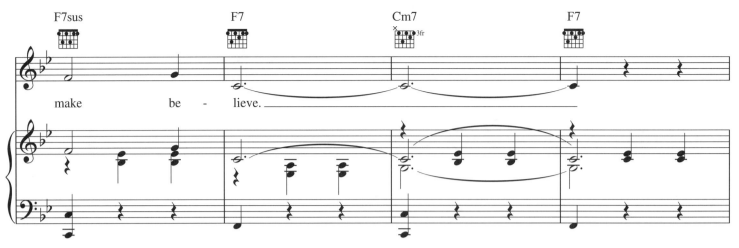

make be - lieve. _____

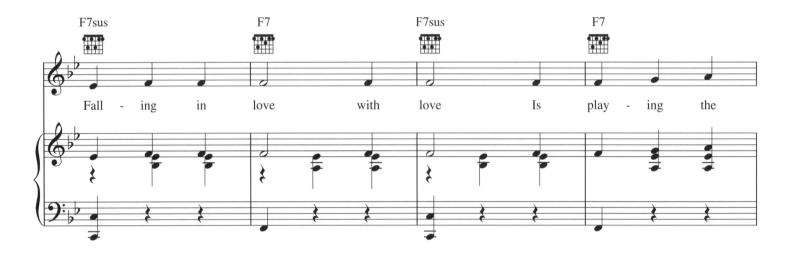

Fall - ing in love with love Is play - ing the

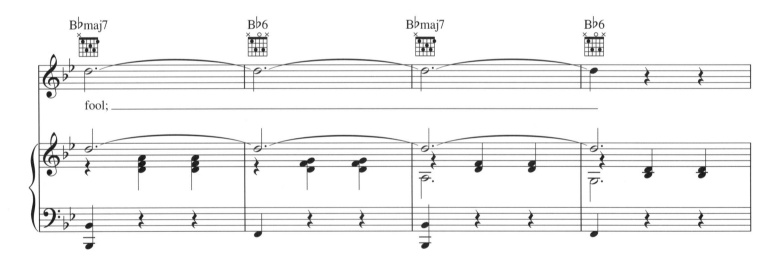

fool; _____

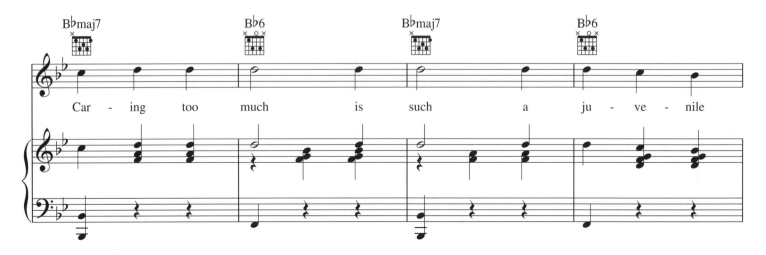

Car - ing too much is such a ju - ve - nile

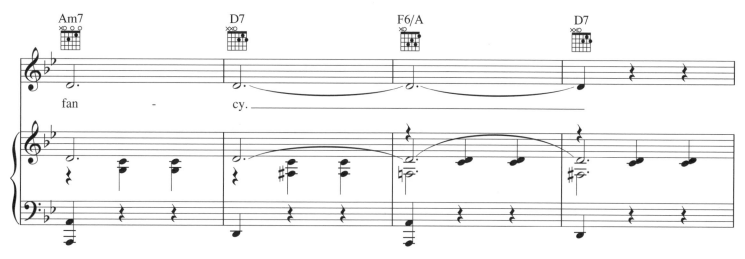

fan - cy.

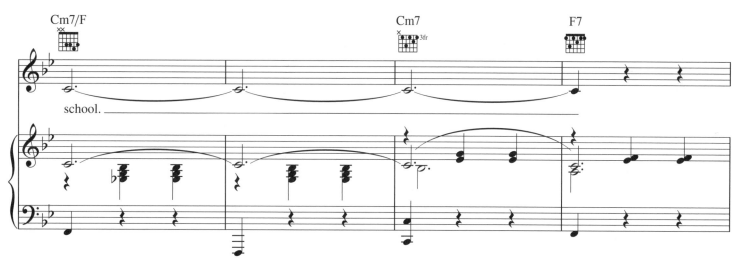

Learn - ing to trust is just For chil - dren in

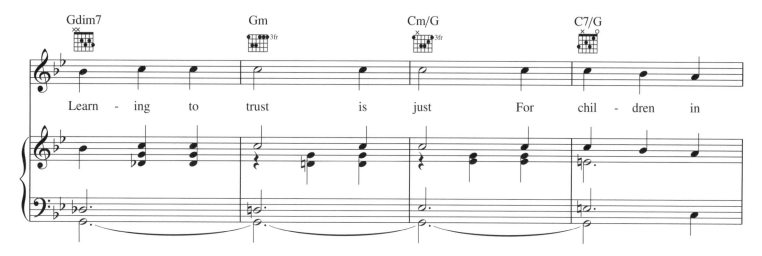

school.

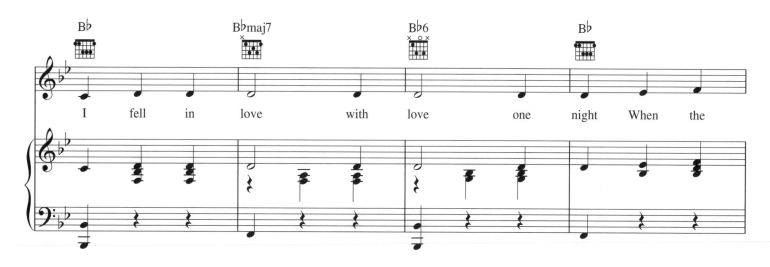

I fell in love with love one night When the

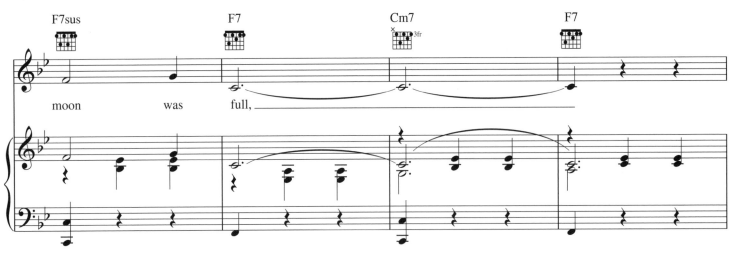

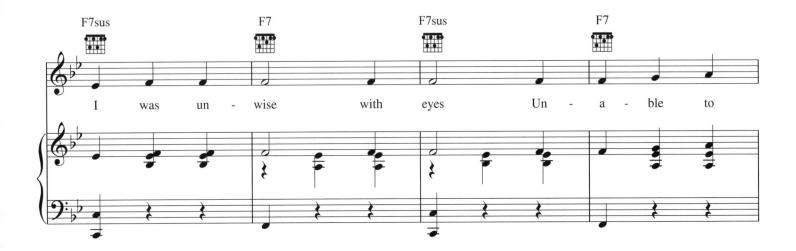

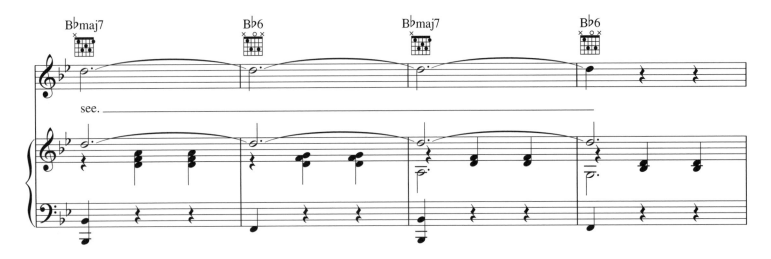

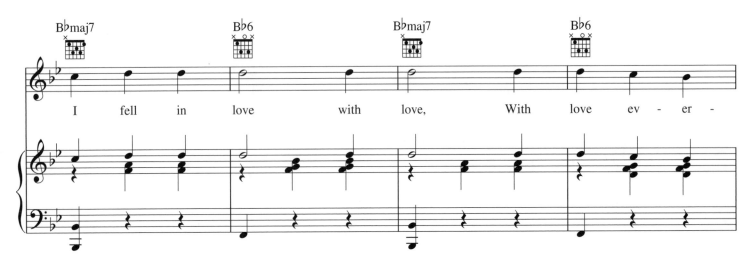

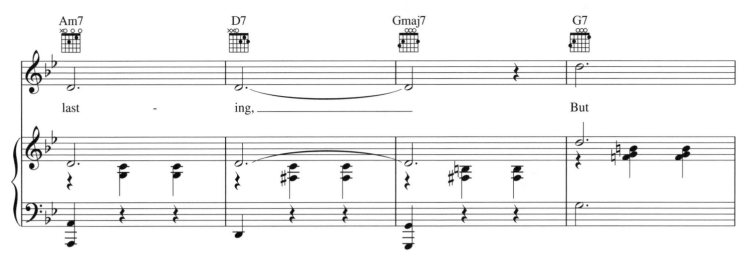

last - ing, _____ But

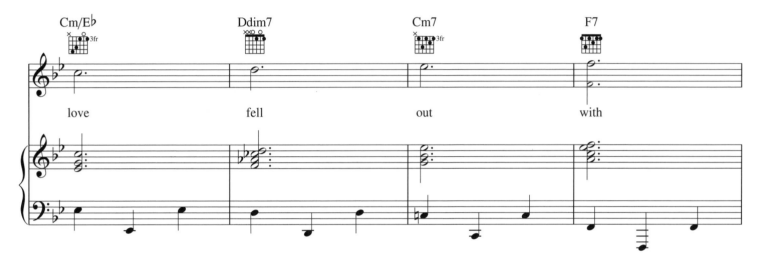

love   fell   out   with

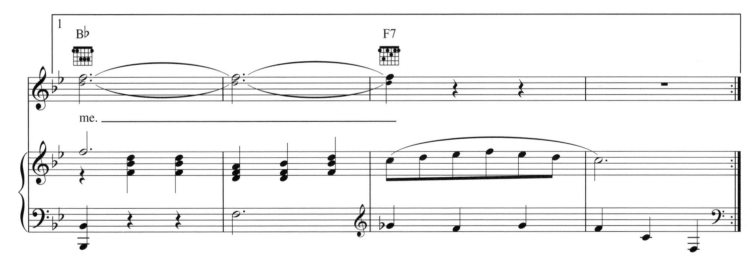

me.

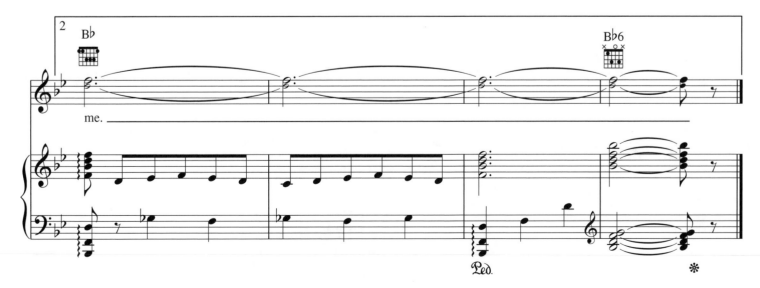

me.

HELLO, YOUNG LOVERS

from THE KING AND I

Lyrics by OSCAR HAMMERSTEIN II
Music by RICHARD RODGERS

Molto moderato

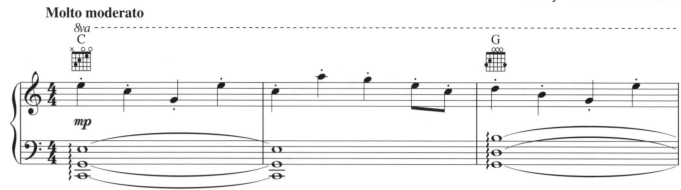

Slowly

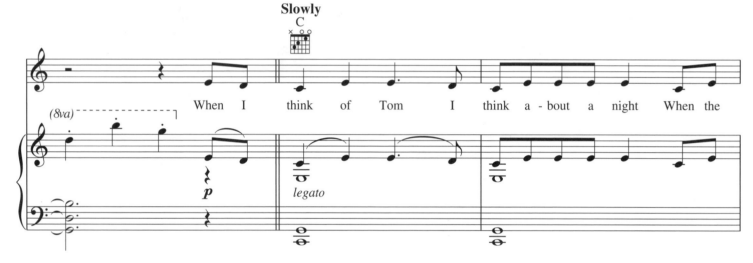

When I think of Tom I think a-bout a night When the

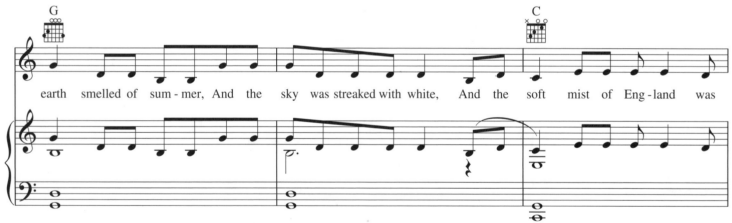

earth smelled of sum-mer, And the sky was streaked with white, And the soft mist of Eng-land was

sleep-ing on a hill; I re-mem-ber this_____ And I al-ways

will. _____ There are new lov-ers now on the

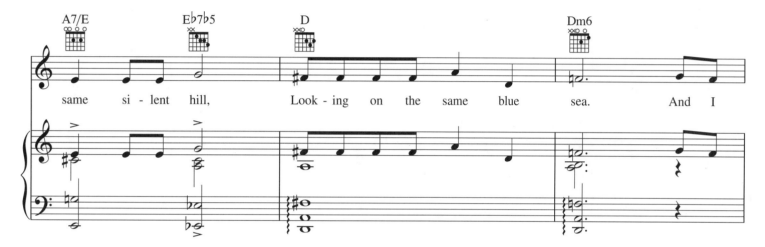

same si-lent hill, Look-ing on the same blue sea. And I

know Tom and I are a part of them all, And they're all a part of Tom _____

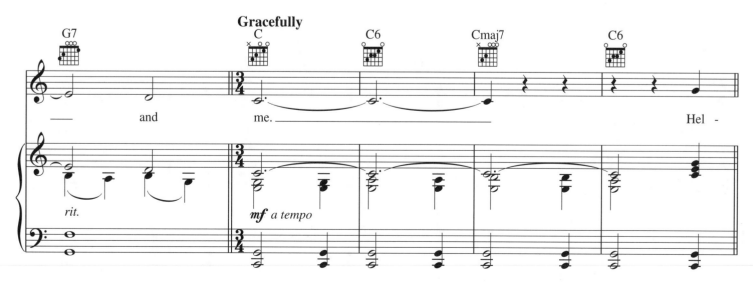

____ and me. _____ Hel -

Refrain *(very moderately)*

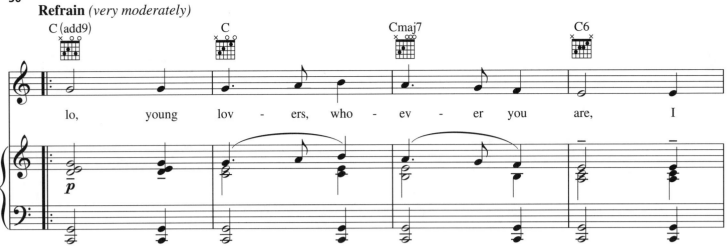

lo, young lov - ers, who - ev - er you are, I

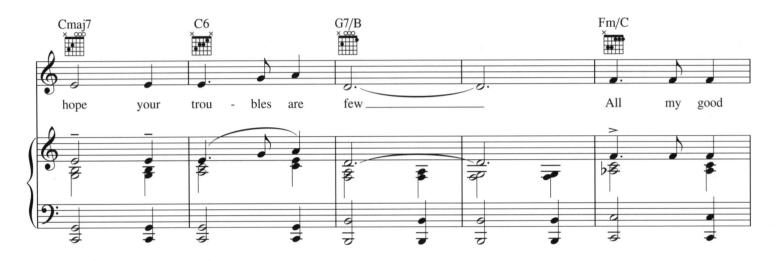

hope your trou - bles are few _____ All my good

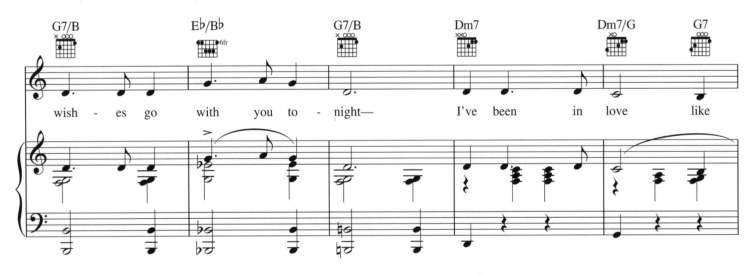

wish - es go with you to - night— I've been in love like

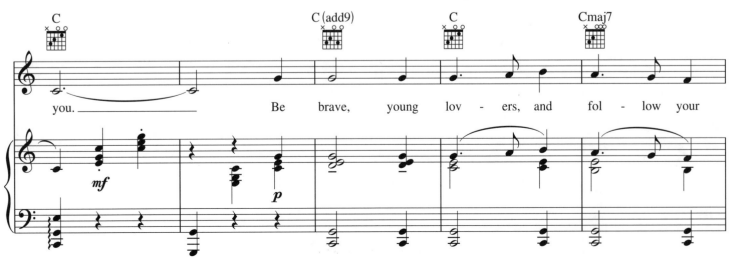

you. _____ Be brave, young lov - ers, and fol - low your

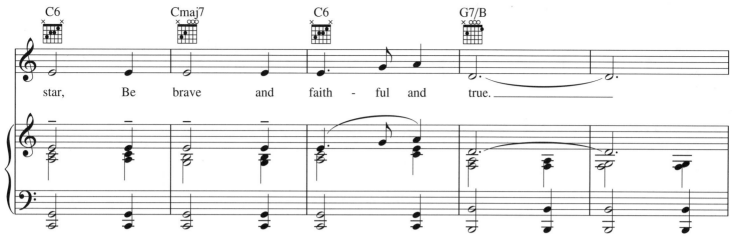

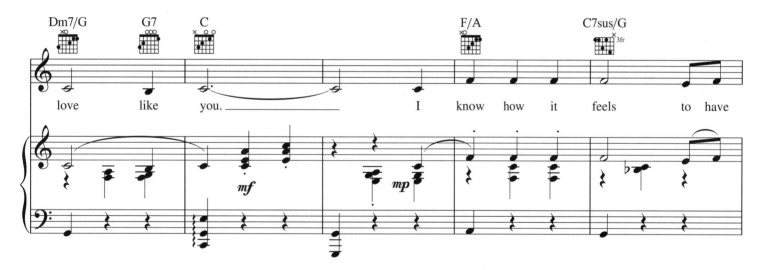

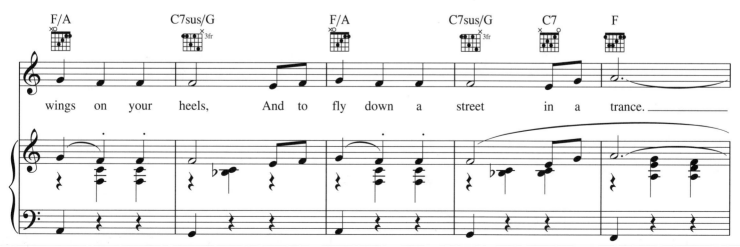

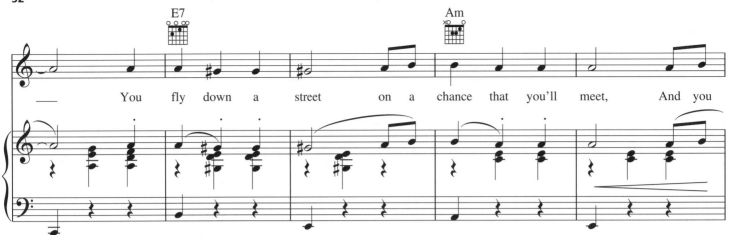

You fly down a street on a chance that you'll meet, And you

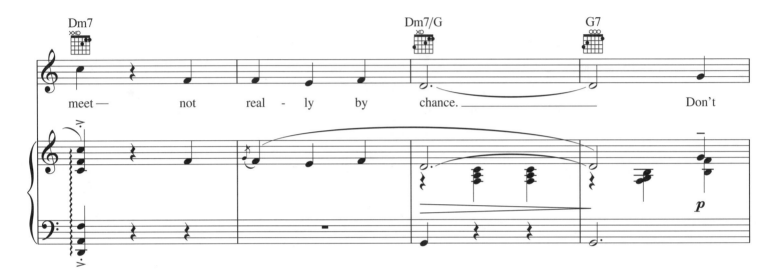

meet — not real-ly by chance. _____ Don't

cry, young lov-ers, What-ev-er you do, Don't cry be-

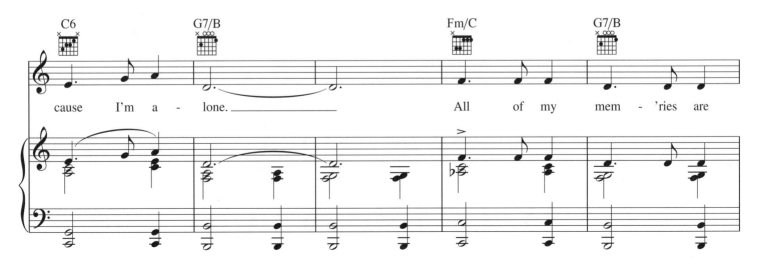

cause I'm a-lone. _____ All of my mem-'ries are

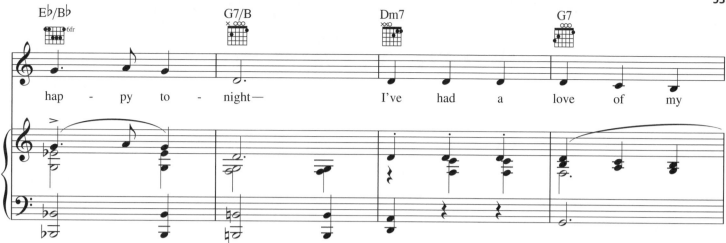

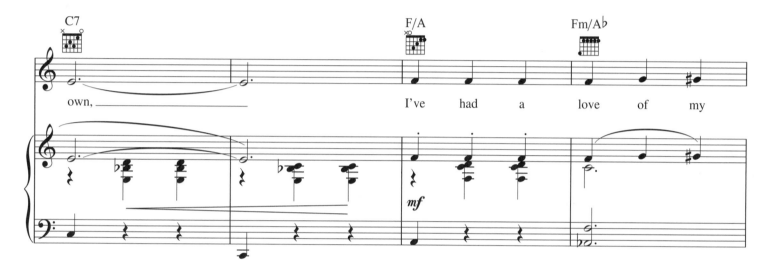

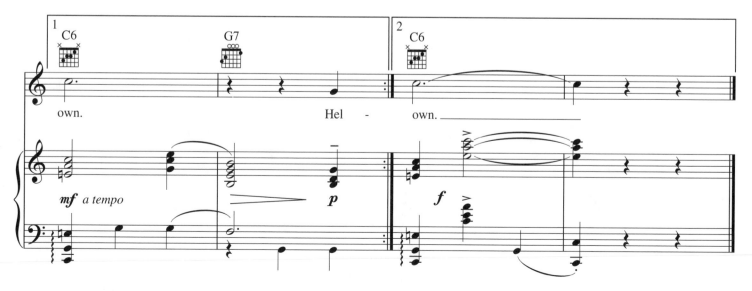

HOW MUCH IS THAT DOGGIE
IN THE WINDOW

Words and Music by
BOB MERRILL

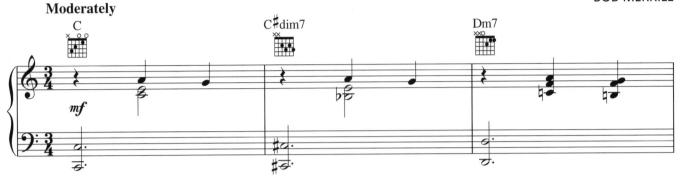

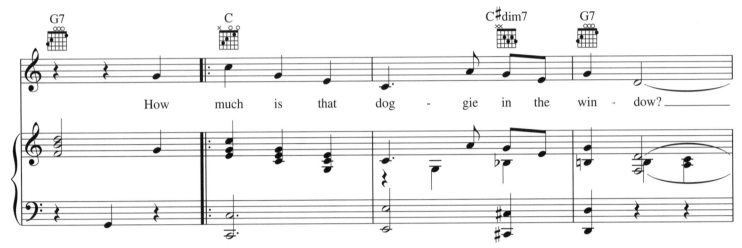

How much is that dog - gie in the win - dow? _____

(Bark,   bark!)

_____ The   one   with   the   wag - gel - y

tail; _____   how   much   is   that   dog - gie   in   the

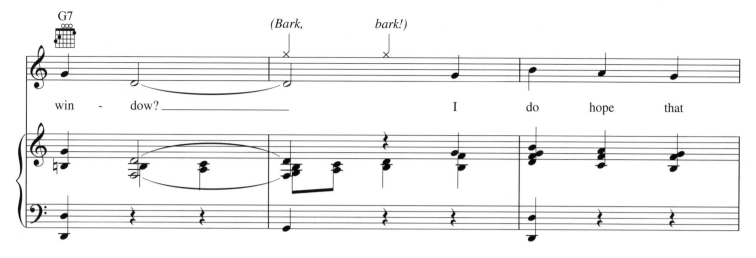

win - dow? _____ (Bark, bark!) I do hope that

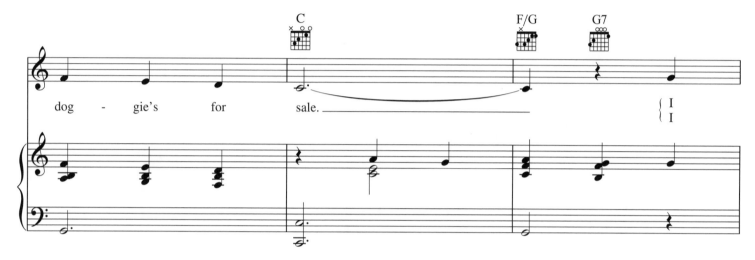

dog - gie's for sale. _____ { I / I

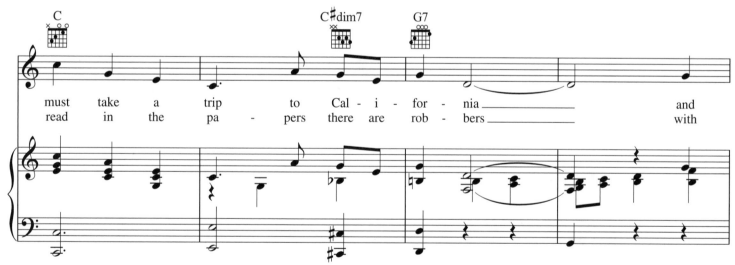

must take a trip to Cal - i - for - nia _____ and
read in the pa - pers there are rob - bers _____ with

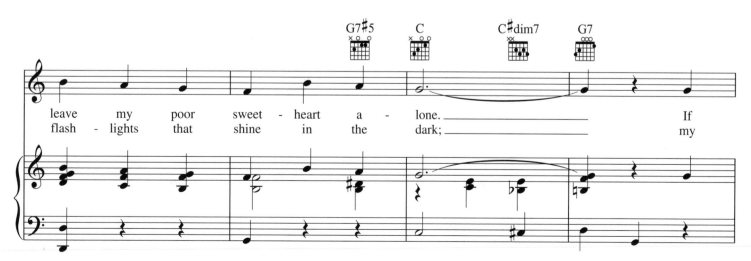

leave my poor sweet - heart a - lone. _____ If
flash - lights poor that shine in the dark; _____ my

he has a dog he won't be lone - some, _____ and the
love needs a dog - gie to pro - tect him _____ and

1

dog - gie will have a good home. _____ How
scare them a - way with one

2

bark. _____ I

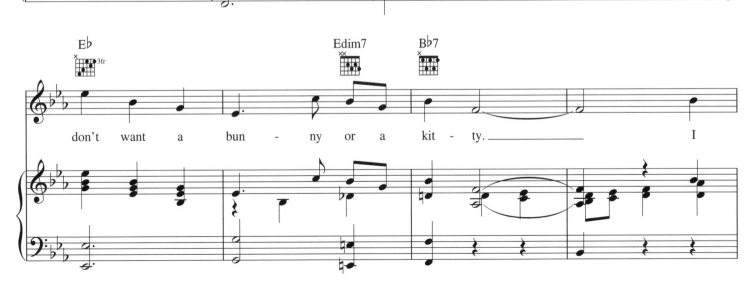

don't want a bun - ny or a kit - ty. _____ I

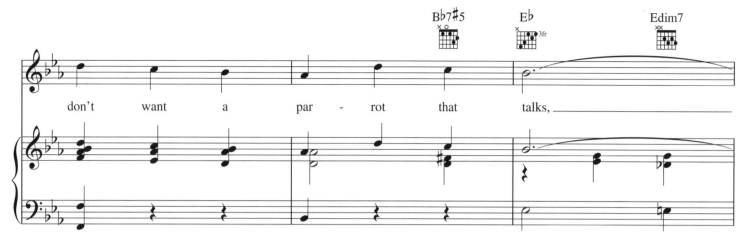

don't want a par - rot that talks, _____

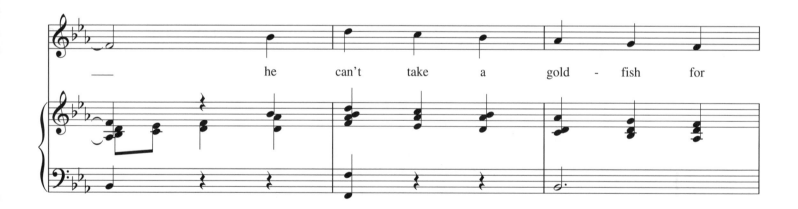

_____ I don't want a bowl of lit - tle fish - ies; _____

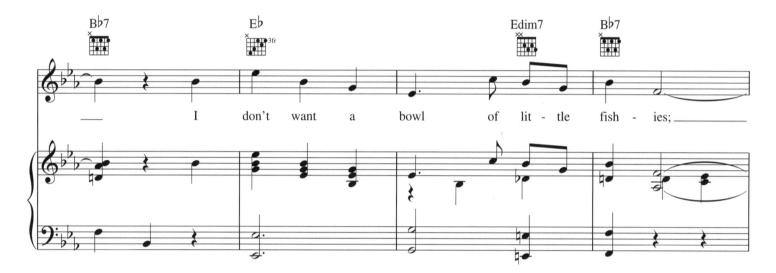

_____ he can't take a gold - fish for

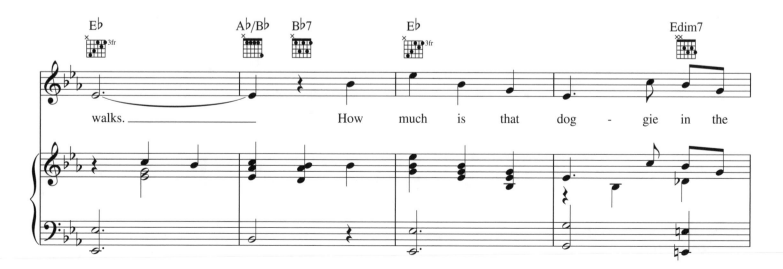

walks. _____ How much is that dog - gie in the

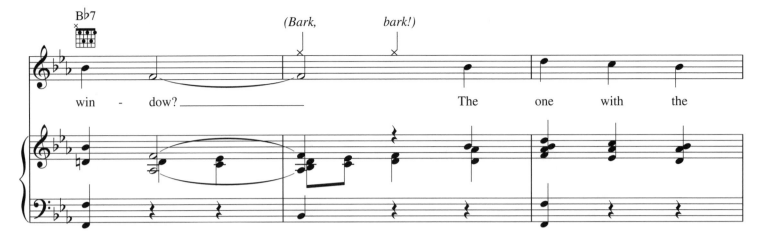

win - dow? _____ The one with the

wag - gel - y tail; _____ how much is that

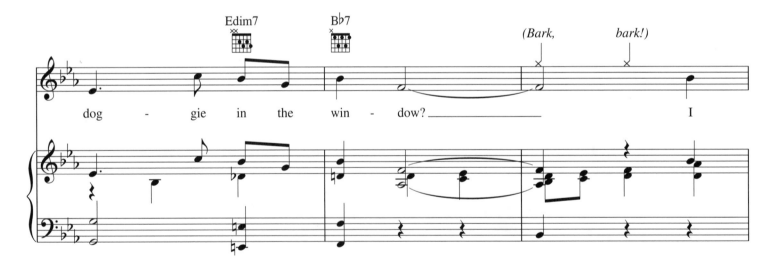

dog - gie in the win - dow? _____ I

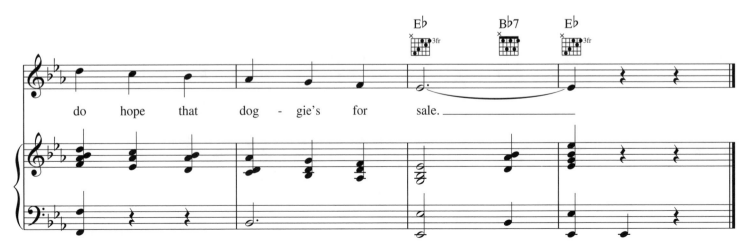

do hope that dog - gie's for sale. _____

I WONDER WHO'S KISSING HER NOW

Lyrics by WILL M. HOUGH and FRANK R. ADAMS
Music by JOSEPH E. HOWARD and HAROLD ORLOB

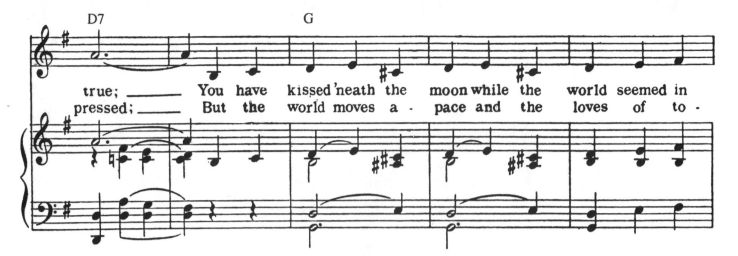

true; _____ You have kissed 'neath the moon while the world seemed in
pressed; _____ But the world moves a - pace and the loves of to -

tune, Then you've left her to hunt a new game, _____ Does it ev - er oc -
day Flit a - way with a smile and a tear, _____ So you nev - er can

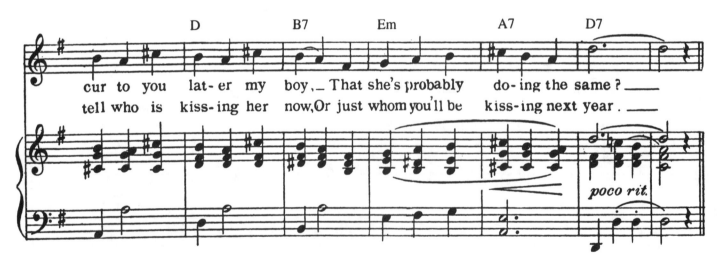

cur to you lat - er my boy, _ That she's probably do - ing the same? _____
tell who is kiss - ing her now, Or just whom you'll be kiss - ing next year. _____

Chorus. G

I won - der who's kiss - ing her now, _____ Won - der who's teach - ing her

now, _____ Won-der who's look-ing in-to her eyes Breath-ing

sighs, tell-ing lies; I won-der who's buy-ing the wine, _____ For

poco rit.   *a tempo.*

lips that I used to call mine. _____ Won-der if she ev-er tells him of

allargamente.

me, I won-der who's kissing her now. _____ I kiss-ing her now _____

f   *rall.*   *p*   *a tempo.*

I'LL TAKE ROMANCE

Lyrics by OSCAR HAMMERSTEIN II
Music by BEN OAKLAND

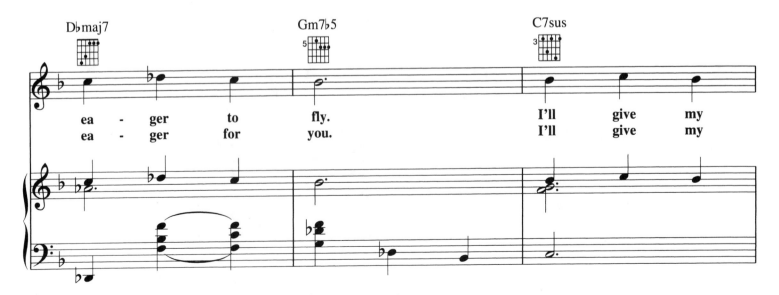

IF YOU GO AWAY

French Words and Music by JACQUES BREL
English Words by ROD McKUEN

Slowly, with much feeling

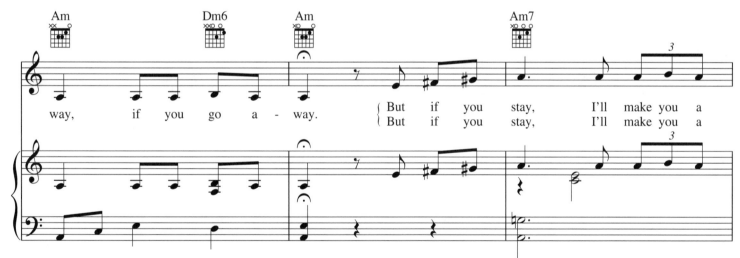

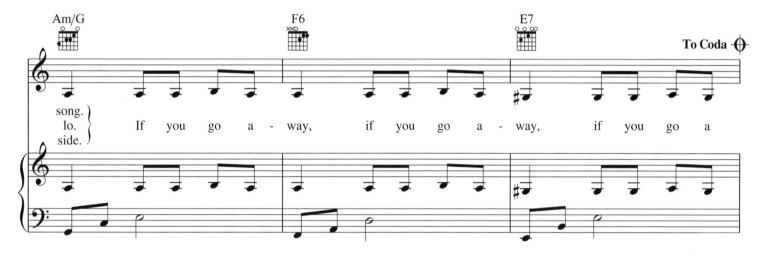

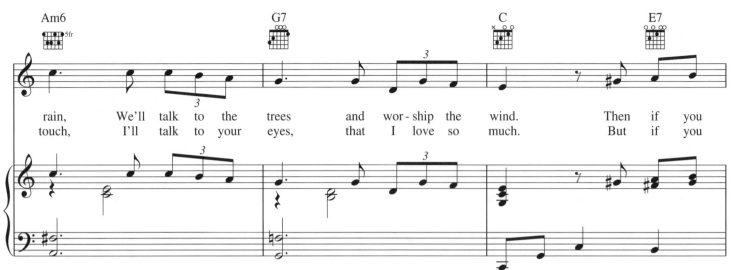

rain, We'll talk to the trees, and wor-ship the wind. Then if you
touch, I'll talk to your eyes, that I love so much. But if you

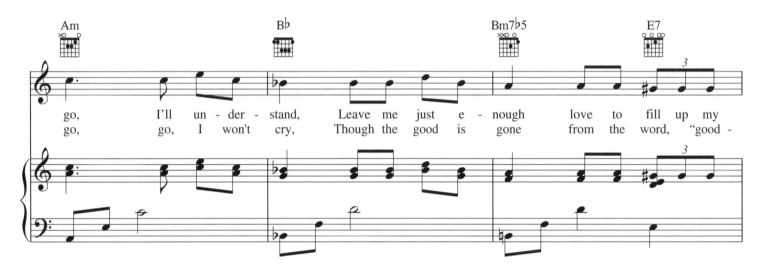

go, I'll un - der - stand, Leave me just e - nough love to fill up my
go, go, I won't cry, Though the good is gone from the word, "good -

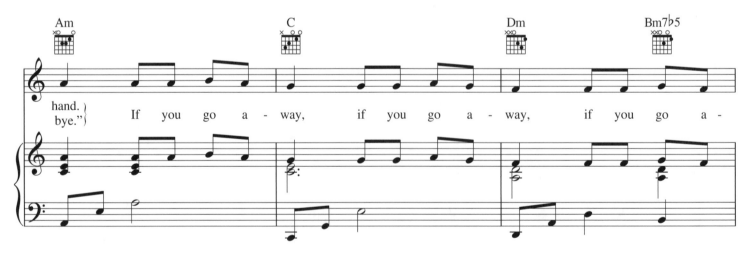

hand. }
bye." } If you go a - way, if you go a - way, if you go a -

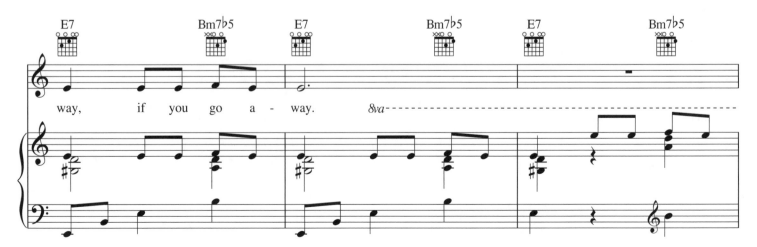

way, if you go a - way. *8va*

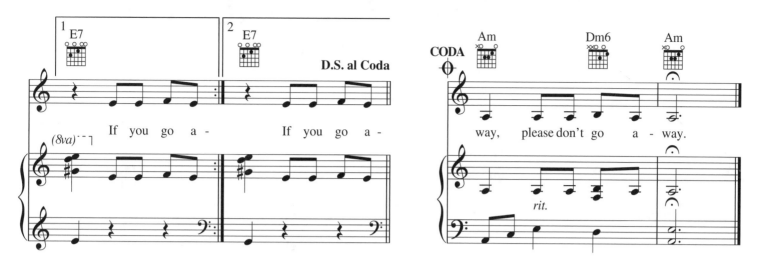

If you go a -   If you go a -

D.S. al Coda

CODA

way,   please don't go a - way.

rit.

Additional Lyrics

1. Ne me quitte pas,
   Il faut oublier
   Tout peut s'oublier
   Qui s'enfuit déjà,
   Oublier le temps
   Des malentendus
   Et le temps perdu
   A savoir comment
   Oublier ces heures
   Qui tuaient parfois
   A coups de pourquoi
   Le coeur du bonheur...
   Ne me quitte pas,
   Ne me quitte pas,
   Ne me quitte pas,
   Ne me quitte pas.

2. Moi je t'offrirai
   Des perles de pluie
   Venues de pays
   Ou il ne pleut pas;
   Je creusrai la terre
   Jusqu'après me mort
   Pour couvrir ton corps
   D'or et de lumière;
   Je f'rai un domaine
   Ou l'amour s'ra roi
   Ou l'amour s'ra roi
   Ou tu seras reine
   Ne me quitte pas,
   Ne me quitte pas,
   Ne me quitte pas,
   Ne me quitte pas.

3. Ne me quitte pas,
   Je t'inventerai
   Des mots insenses
   Que tu comprendras,
   Je te parlerai
   De ces amants là
   Qui ont vû deux fois
   Leurs coeurs s'embraser,
   Je te racont'rai
   L'histoire de ce roi
   Mort de n'avoir pas
   Pu te rencontrer
   Ne me quitte pas,
   Ne me quitte pas,
   Ne me quitte pas,
   Ne me quitte pas.

4. On a vu souvent
   Rejaillir le feu
   De l'ancien volcan
   Qu'on croyait trop vieux;
   Il est, parait-il,
   Des terres brulées
   Donnant plus de blé
   Qu'un meilleur avril,
   Et quand vient le soir
   Pour qu'un ciel flamboie
   Le rouge et le noir
   Ne s'epous'nt ils pas
   Ne me quitte pas,
   Ne me quitte pas,
   Ne me quitte pas,
   Ne me quitte pas.

5. Ne me quitte pas,
   Je n'vais plus pleurer
   Je n'vais plus parler,
   Je me cach'rai la
   A te regarder
   Causer et sourire
   Et a t'écouter
   Chanter et puis rire;
   Laiss'moi de venir
   L'ombre de ton ombre,
   L'ombre de ta main,
   L'ombre de ton chien;
   Ne me quitte pas,
   Ne me quitte pas,
   Ne me quitte pas,
   Ne me quitte pas.

IF YOU WERE THE ONLY GIRL IN THE WORLD

Words by CLIFFORD GREY
Music by NAT D. AYER

IT'S A GRAND NIGHT FOR SINGING

from STATE FAIR

Lyrics by OSCAR HAMMERSTEIN II
Music by RICHARD RODGERS

Tempo di Valse

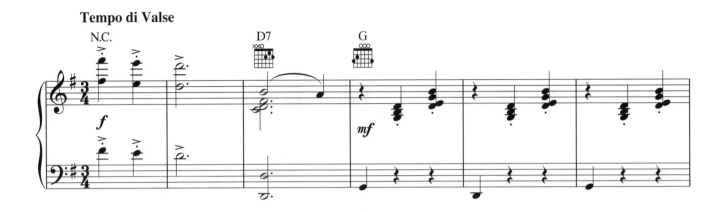

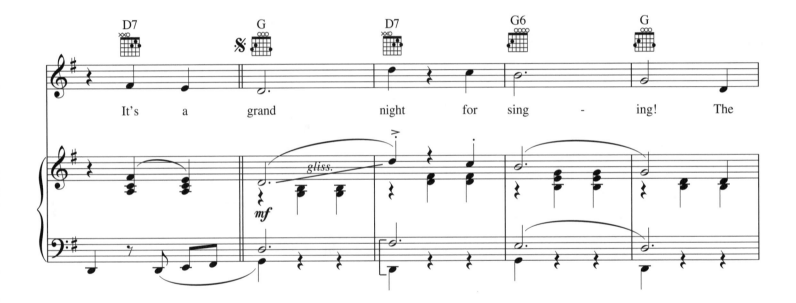

It's a grand night for sing - ing! The

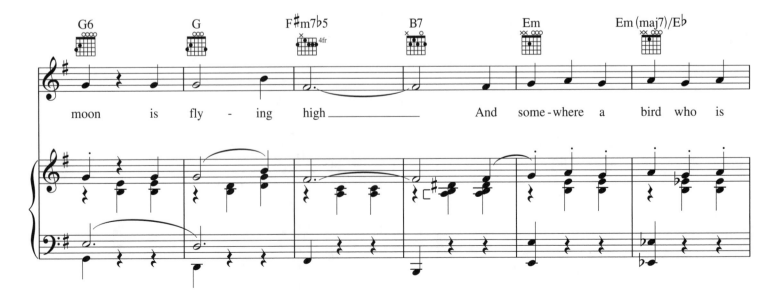

moon is fly - ing high _____ And some - where a bird who is

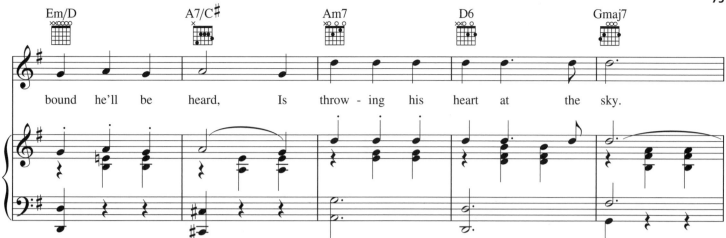

bound he'll be heard, Is throw-ing his heart at the sky.

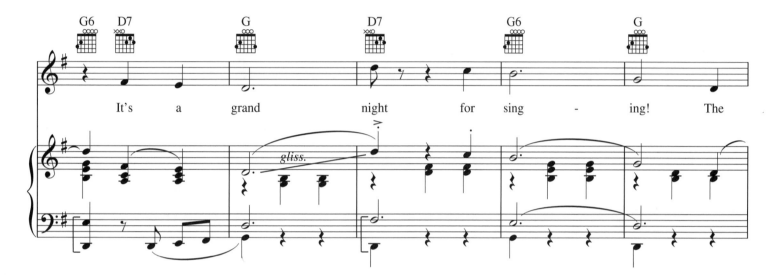

It's a grand night for sing - ing! The

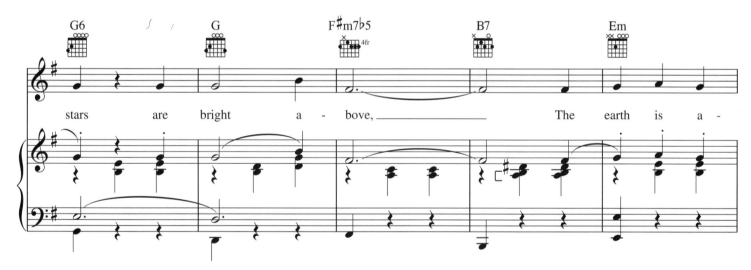

stars are bright a - bove, _____ The earth is a -

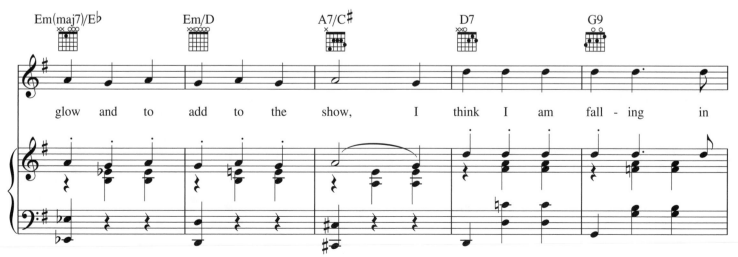

glow and to add to the show, I think I am fall-ing in

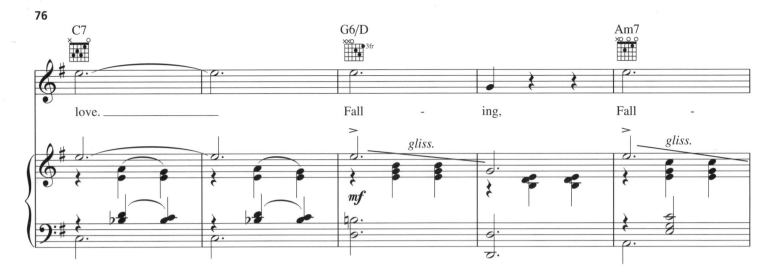

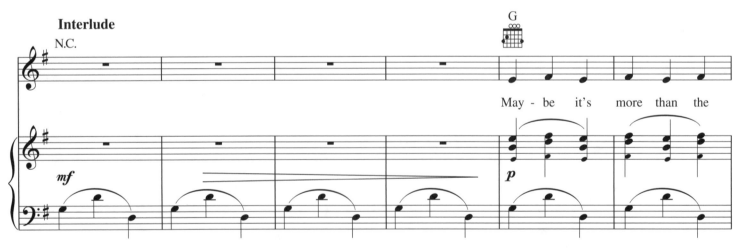

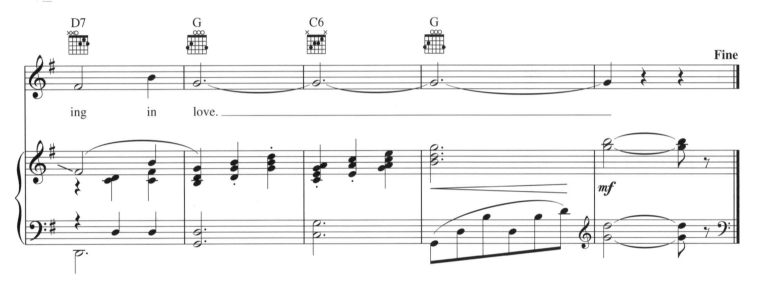

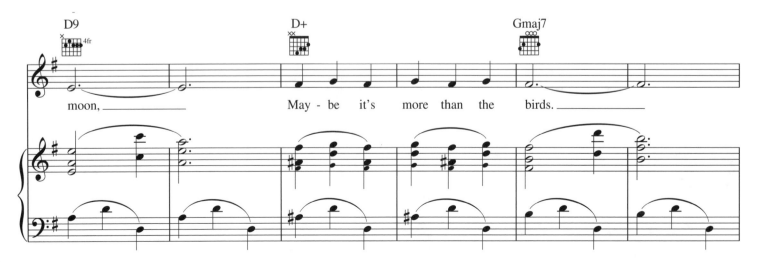

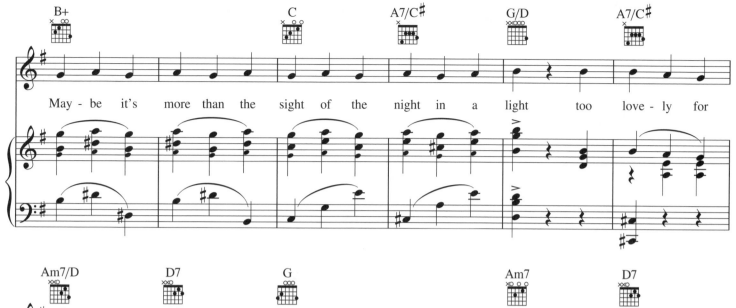

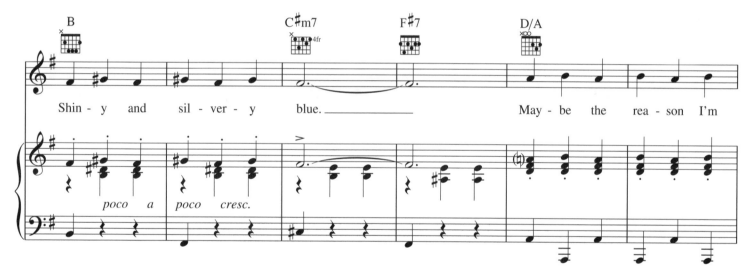

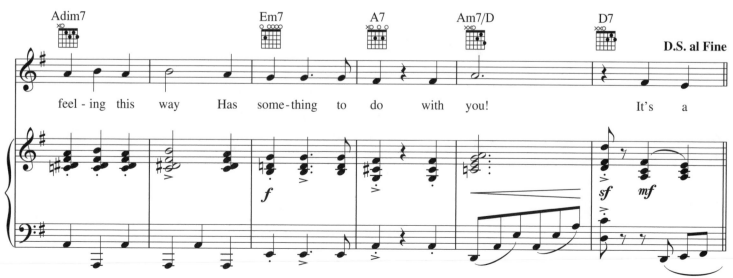

IT'S ALMOST TOMORROW

Words and Music by WADE BUFF
and GENE ADKINSON

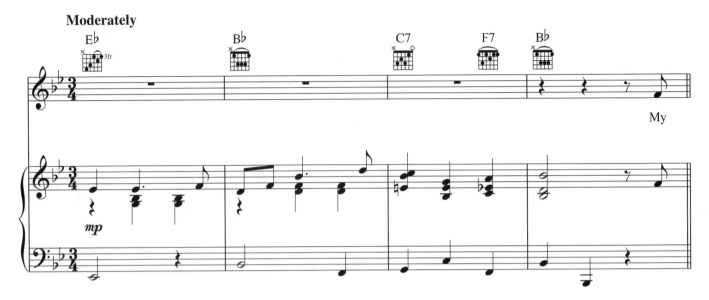

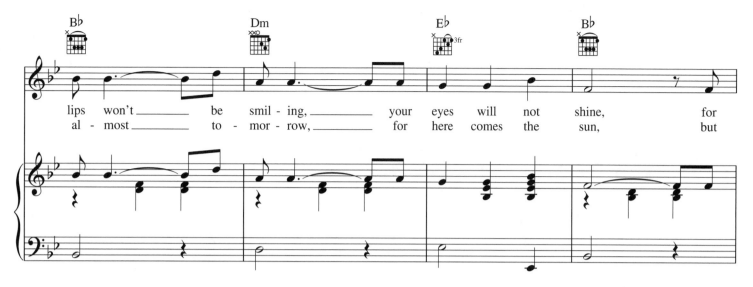

lips won't _____ be smil - ing, _____ your eyes will not shine, for
al - most _____ to - mor - row, _____ for here comes the sun, but

I know to - mor - row that your love won't be mine. }
still I am hop - ing that to - mor - row won't come. }

It's

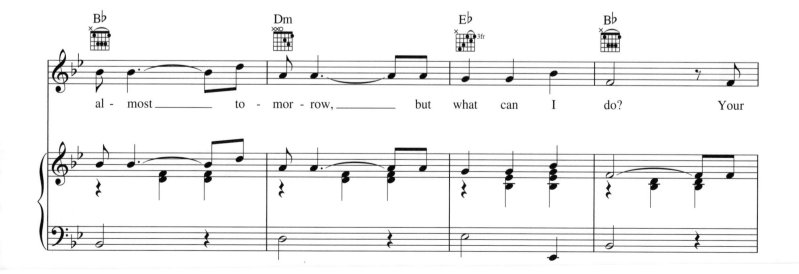

al - most _____ to - mor - row, _____ but what can I do? Your

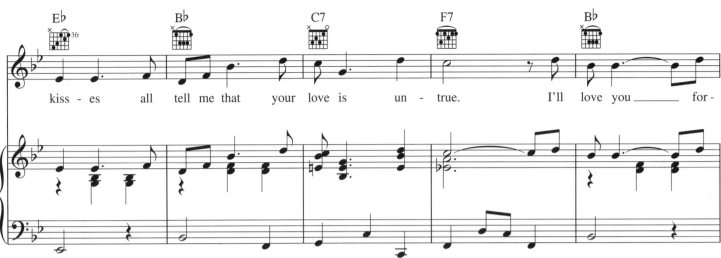

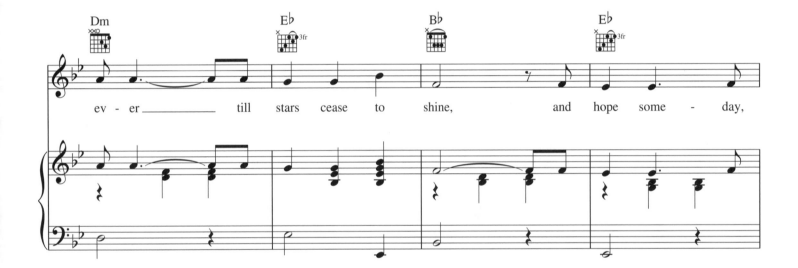

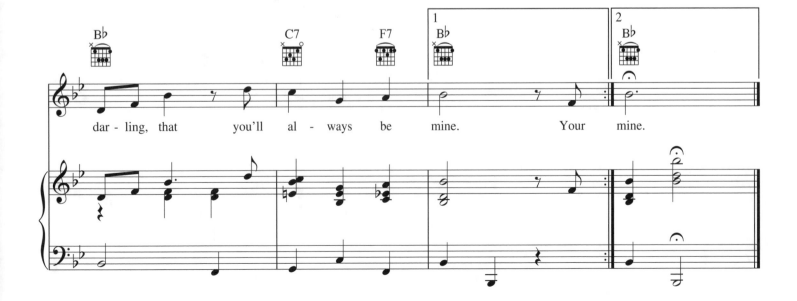

LET ME CALL YOU SWEETHEART

Medium Waltz tempo

Words by BETH SLATER WHITSON
Music by LEO FRIEDMAN

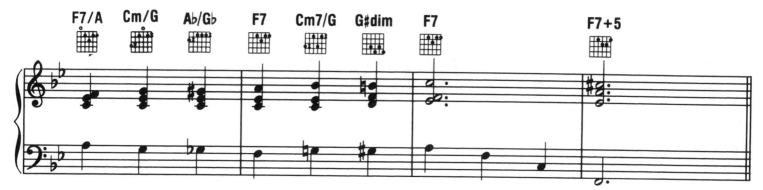

I am dream - ing, dear, of you
Long - ing for you dear all the while

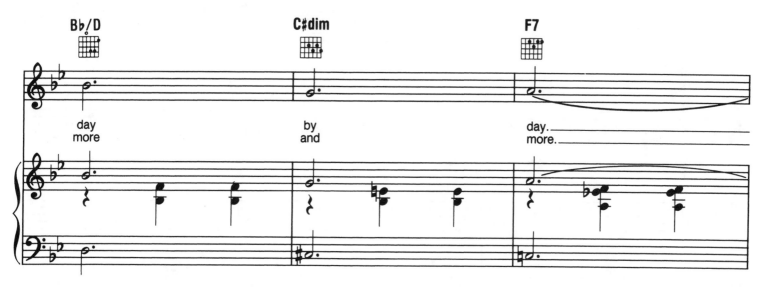

day more by and day. more.

LET'S TAKE
AN OLD-FASHIONED WALK

from the Stage Production MISS LIBERTY

Words and Music by
IRVING BERLIN

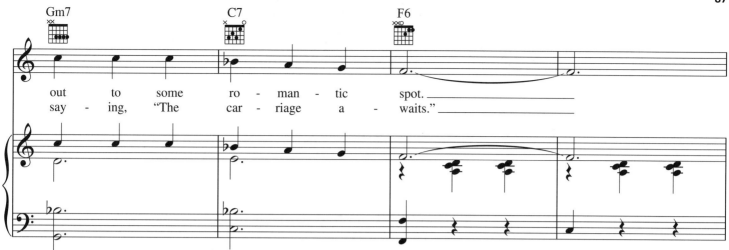

out to some ro - man - tic spot. _____
say - ing, "The car - riage a - waits." _____

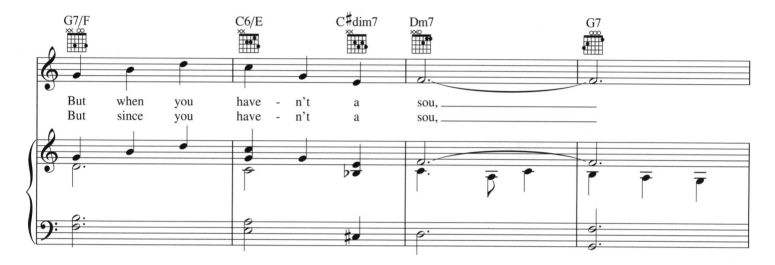

But when you have - n't a sou, _____
But since you have - n't a sou, _____

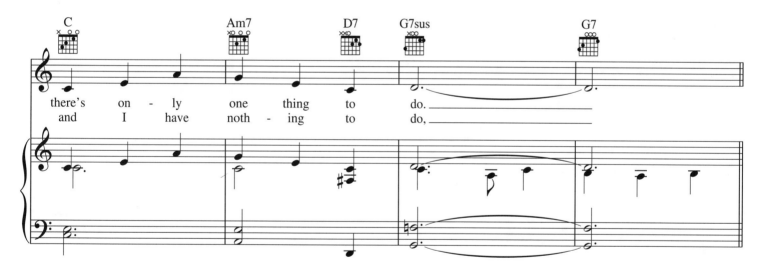

there's on - ly one thing to do. _____
and I have noth - ing to do, _____

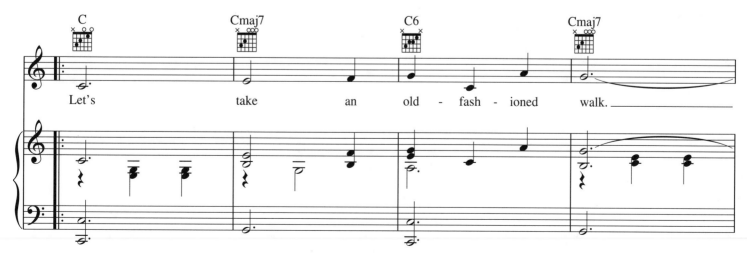

Let's take an old - fash - ioned walk. _____

I'm just burst - ing with talk. _____ What a

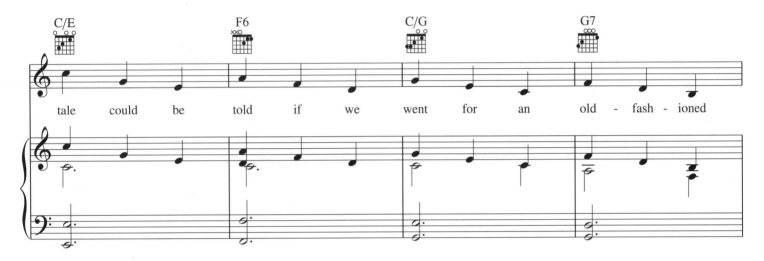

tale could be told if we went for an old - fash - ioned

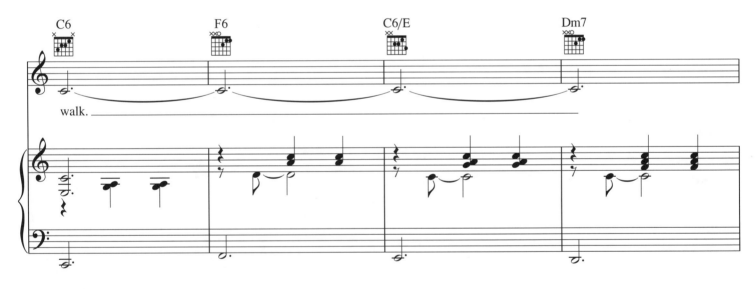

walk. _____

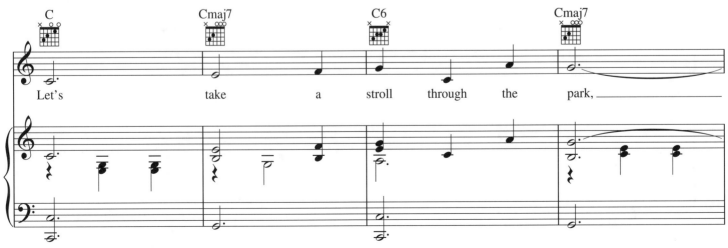

Let's take a stroll through the park, _____

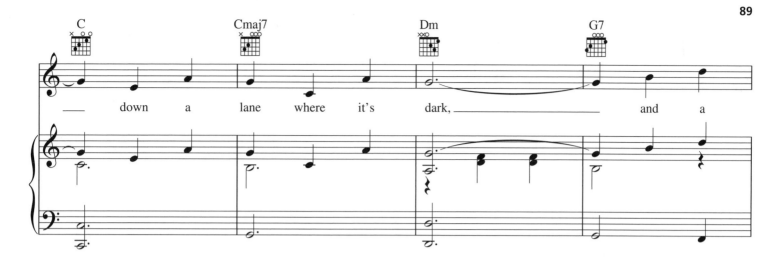

down a lane where it's dark, _____ and a

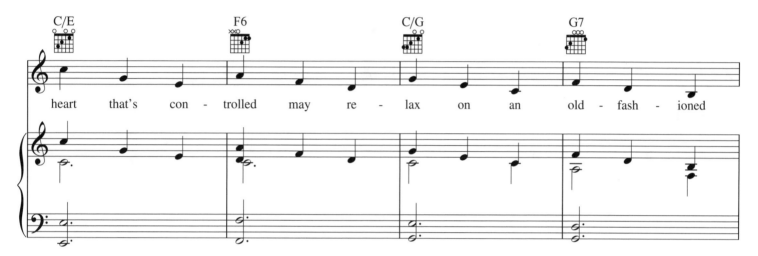

heart that's con - trolled may re - lax on an old - fash - ioned

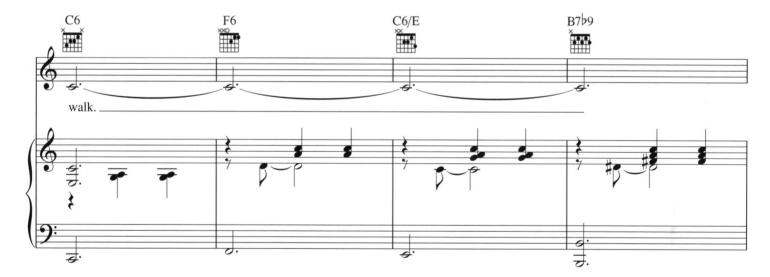

walk. _____

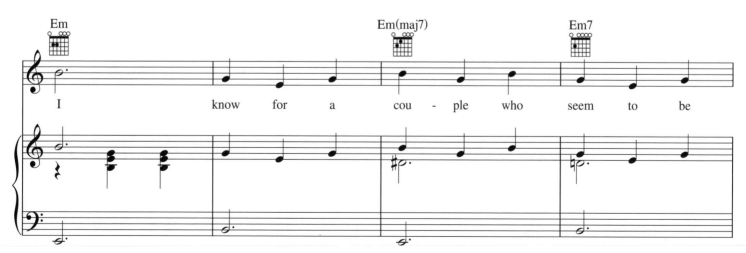

I know for a cou - ple who seem to be

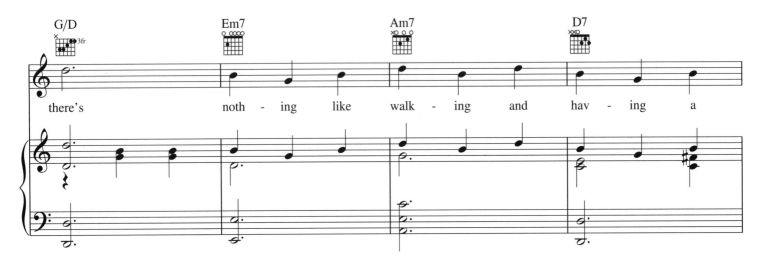

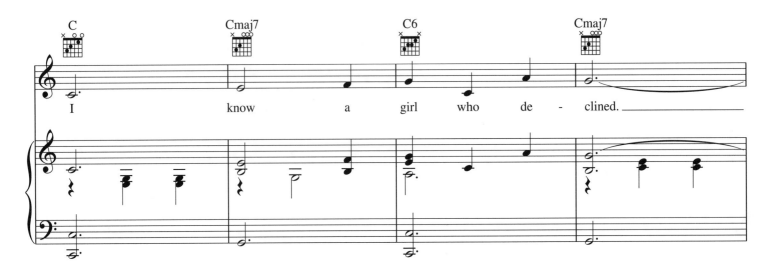

Could - n't make up her mind. _____ She was

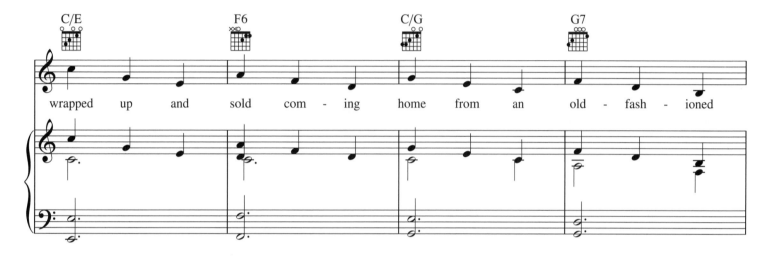

wrapped up and sold com - ing home from an old - fash - ioned

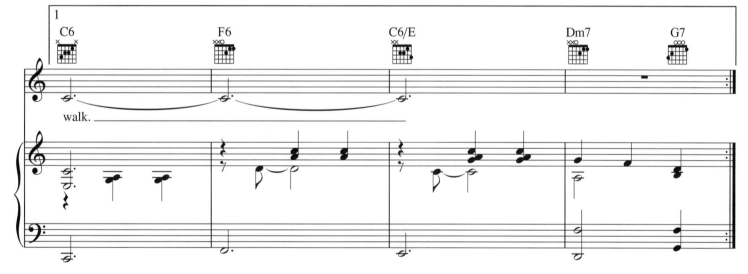

walk. _____

walk. _____

LOLLIPOPS AND ROSES

Words and Music by
TONY VELONA

lol - li - pops and lol - li - pops and ros - es.
lol - li - pops and lol - li - pops and ros - es. We try _____

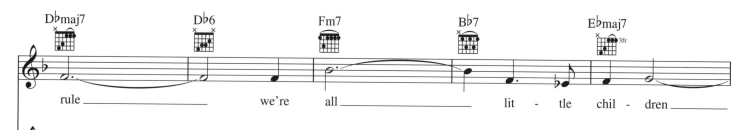

_____ act - ing grown up, _____ but _____ as a

rule _____ we're all _____ lit - tle chil - dren _____

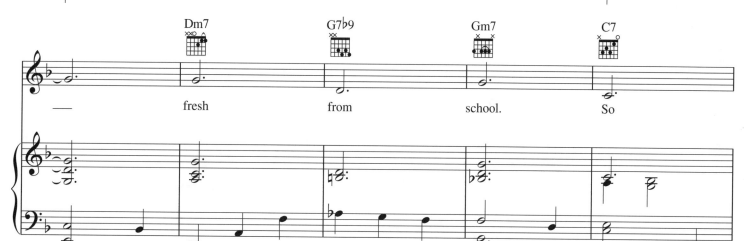

_____ fresh from school. So

LOOK TO THE RAINBOW
from FINIAN'S RAINBOW

Words by E.Y. HARBURG
Music by BURTON LANE

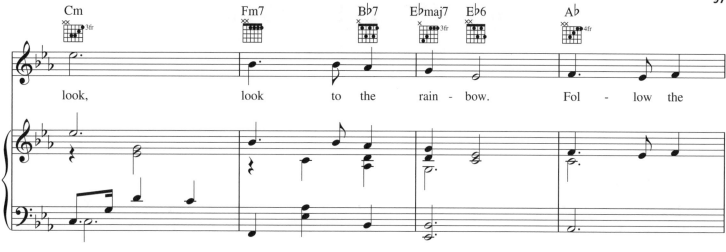

look, look to the rain - bow. Fol - low the

fel - low who fol - lows a dream." {'Twas a dream."
{So I dream."

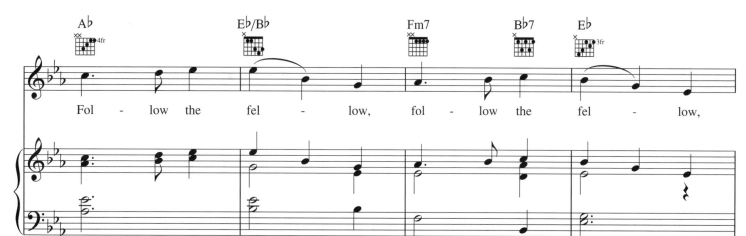

Fol - low the fel - low, fol - low the fel - low,

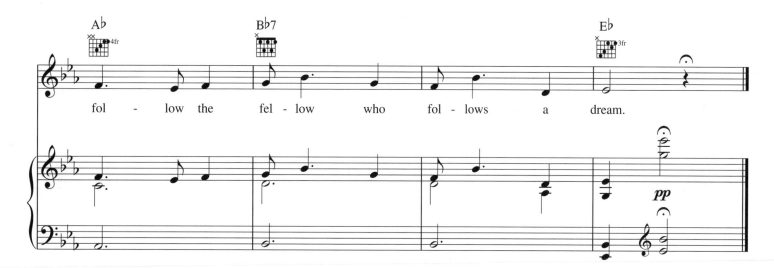

fol - low the fel - low who fol - lows a dream.

MEXICALI ROSE

from MEXICALI ROSE

Words by HELEN STONE
Music by JACK B. TENNEY

Mex - i - cal - i Rose, stop cry - ing;

I'll come back to you some sun - ny day.

MOON RIVER
from the Paramount Picture BREAKFAST AT TIFFANY'S

Words by JOHNNY MERCER
Music by HENRY MANCINI

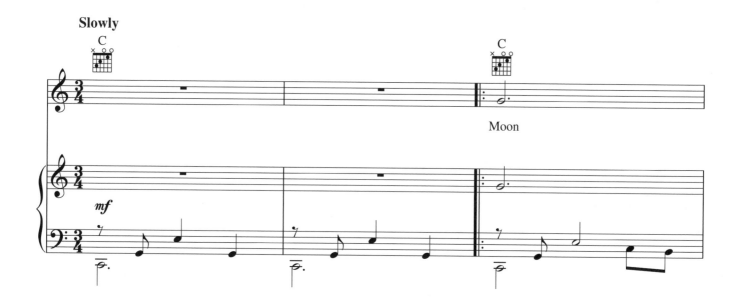

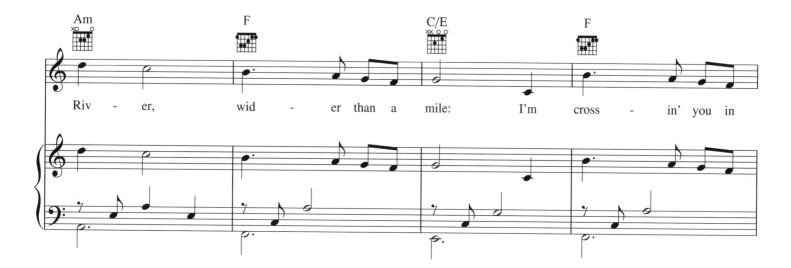

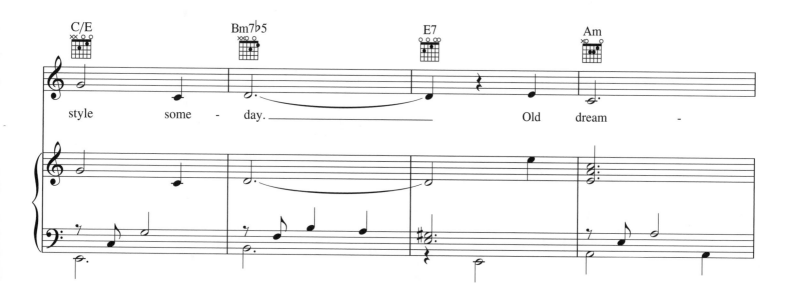

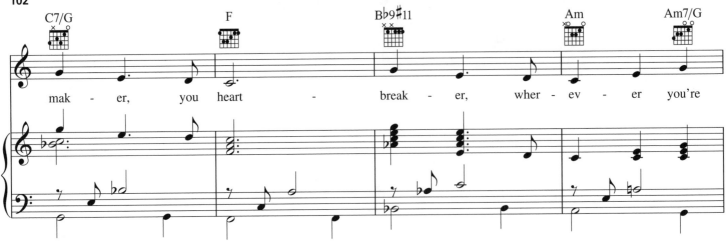

mak - er, you heart - break - er, wher - ev - er you're

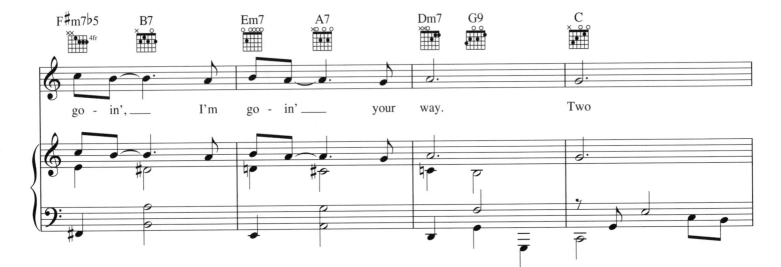

go - in', ___ I'm go - in' ___ your way. Two

drift - ers, off to see the world. There's such a lot of

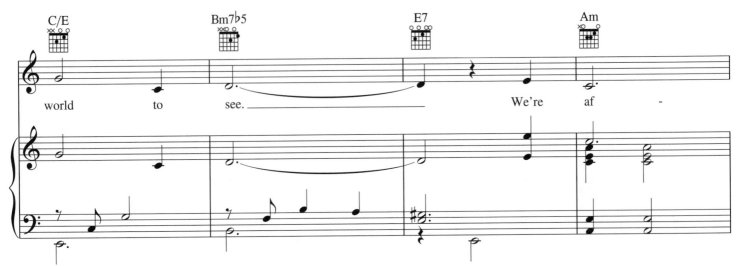

world to see. ___ We're af -

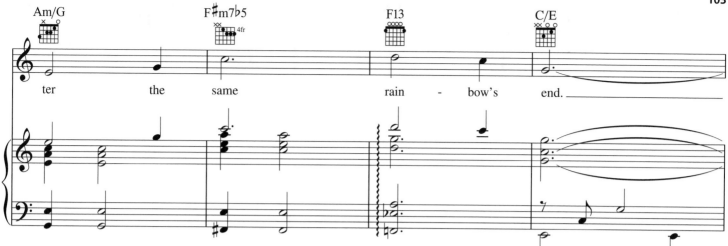

ter the same rain - bow's end. _____

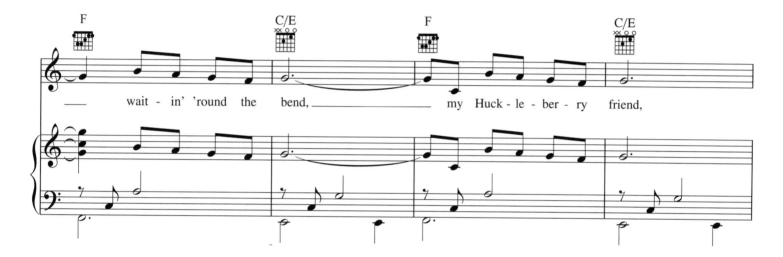

___ wait - in' 'round the bend, _____ my Huck - le - ber - ry friend,

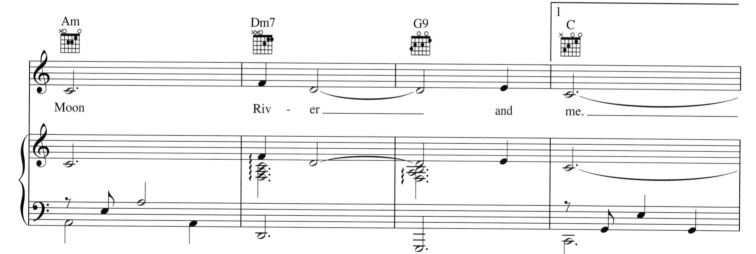

Moon Riv - er _____ and me. _____

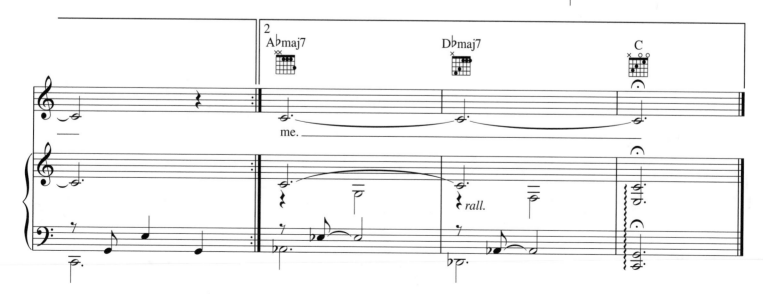

___ me. _____

THE MOST BEAUTIFUL GIRL IN THE WORLD

from JUMBO

Words by LORENZ HART
Music by RICHARD RODGERS

Moderate Waltz tempo

Now the sea - son has a

rea - son, And there's spring - time in my heart.

The most beau - ti - ful girl in the world _____ Picks my

109

MY CUP RUNNETH OVER

from I DO! I DO!

Words by TOM JONES
Music by HARVEY SCHMIDT

Some - times in the morn - ing when shad - ows are
times in the eve - 'ning when you do not

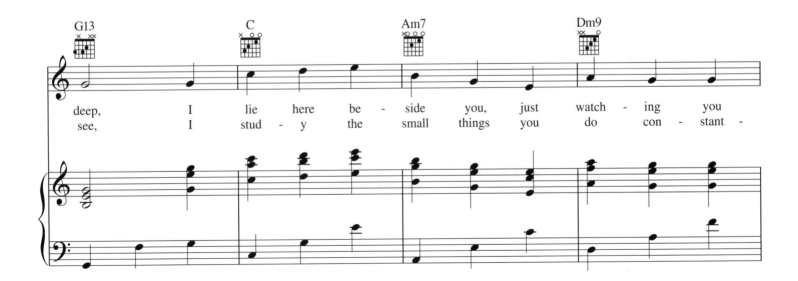

deep, I lie here be - side you, just watch - ing you
see, I stud - y the small things you do con - stant -

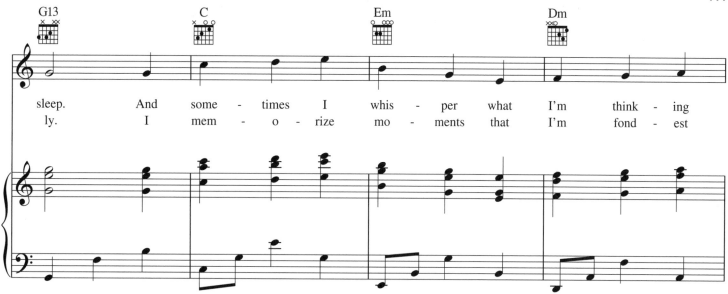

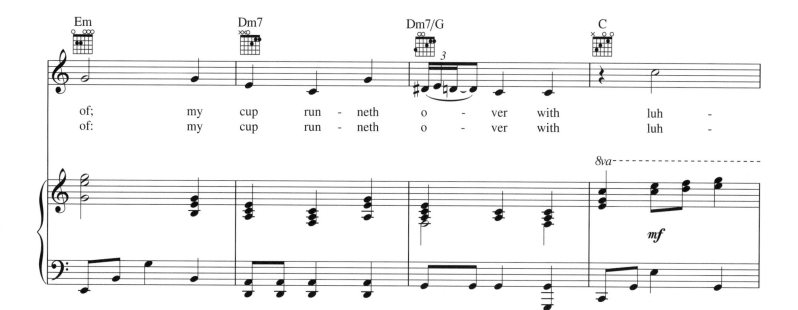

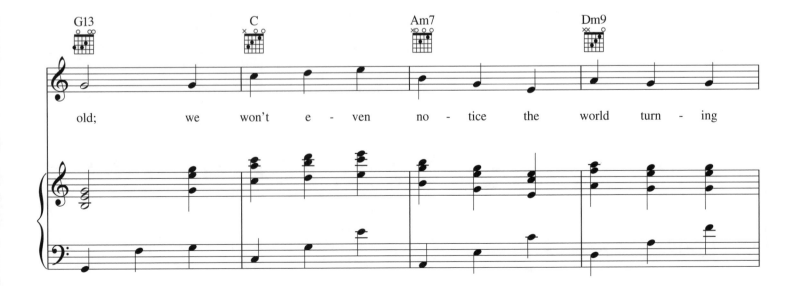

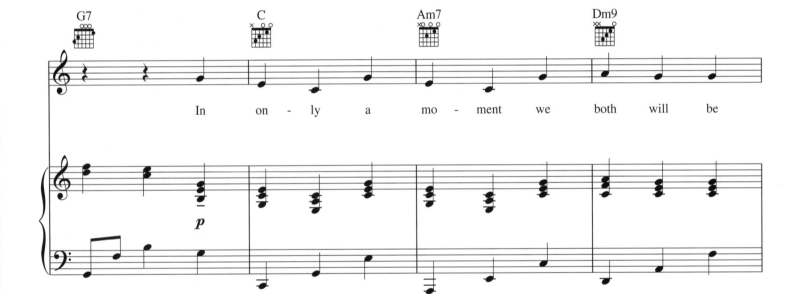

cold. And so in this mo - ment with sun - light a -

bove, my cup run - neth o - ver with luh -

uh - uh - uv, with luh - uh -

uh - uv!

MY FAVORITE THINGS

from THE SOUND OF MUSIC

Lyrics by OSCAR HAMMERSTEIN II
Music by RICHARD RODGERS

OH, WHAT A BEAUTIFUL MORNIN'
from OKLAHOMA!

Lyrics by OSCAR HAMMERSTEIN II
Music by RICHARD RODGERS

Moderate Waltz

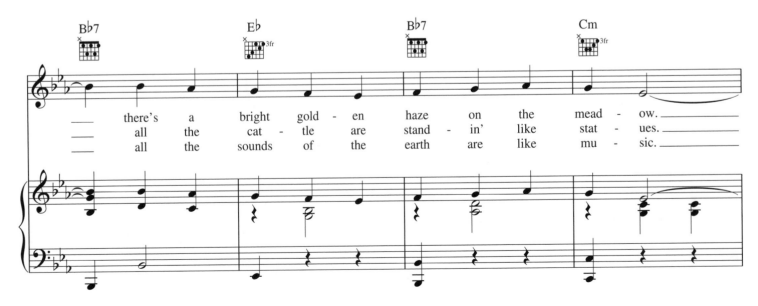

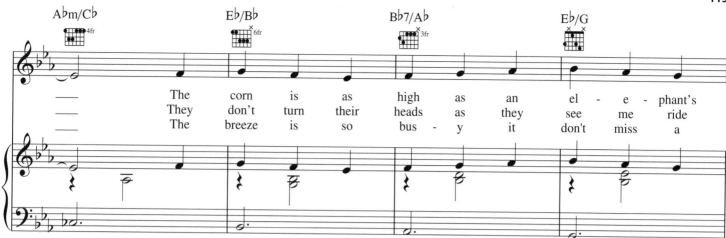

The corn is as high as an el - e - phant's
They don't turn their heads as they see me ride
The breeze is so bus - y it don't miss a

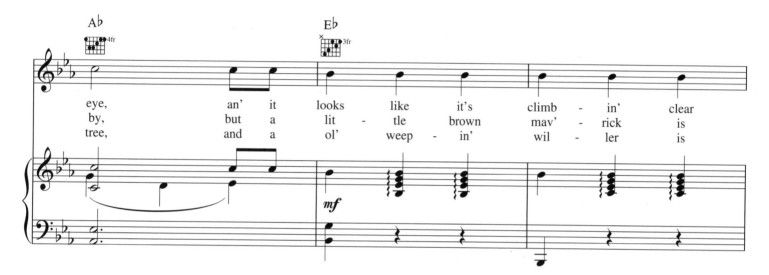

eye, an' it looks like it's climb - in' clear
by, but a lit - tle brown mav' - rick is
tree, and a ol' weep - in' wil - ler is

up to the sky.
wink - in' her eye.
laugh - in' at me!

Oh, what a beau - ti - ful

morn - in'. Oh, what a beau - ti - ful

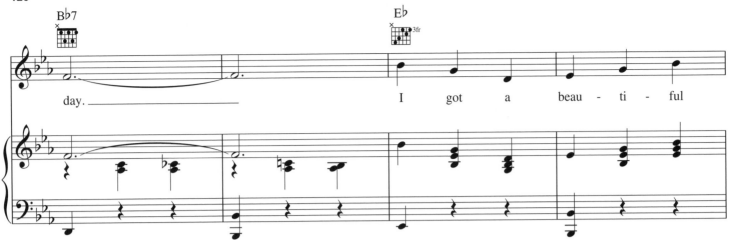

day. _____ I got a beau - ti - ful

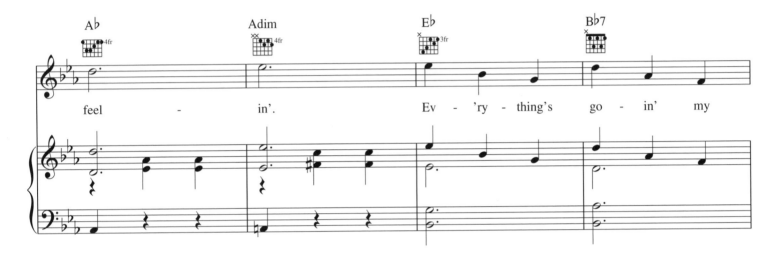

feel - in'. Ev - 'ry - thing's go - in' my

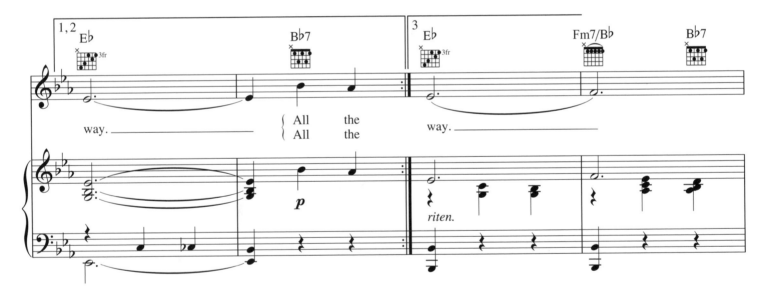

way. _____
{ All the
{ All the way. _____

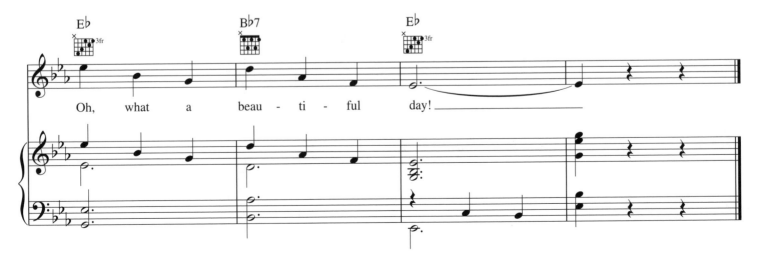

Oh, what a beau - ti - ful day! _____

THE RAINBOW CONNECTION
from THE MUPPET MOVIE

Words and Music by PAUL WILLIAMS
and KENNETH L. ASCHER

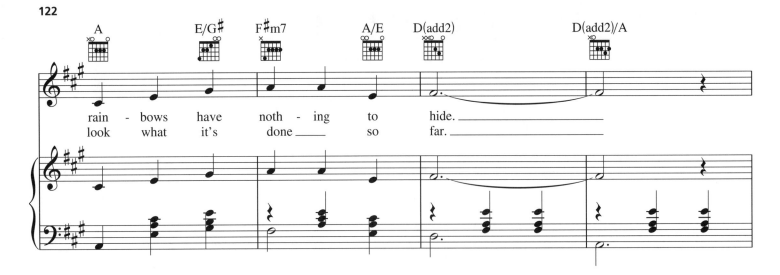

rain - bows have noth - ing to hide. _____
look what it's done _____ so far. _____

So we've been told, and some choose to be - lieve it.
What's so a - maz - ing that keeps us star - gaz - ing, and

I know they're wrong; wait and see. _____
what do we think we might see? _____

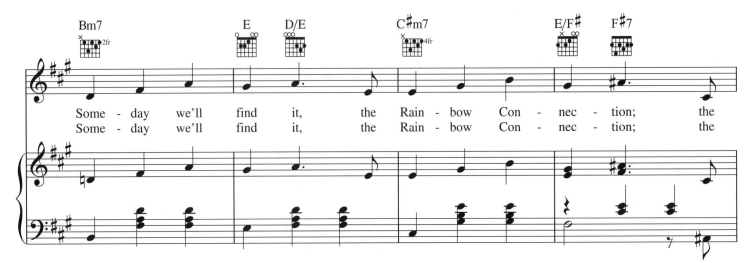

Some - day we'll find it, the Rain - bow Con - nec - tion; the
Some - day we'll find it, the Rain - bow Con - nec - tion; the

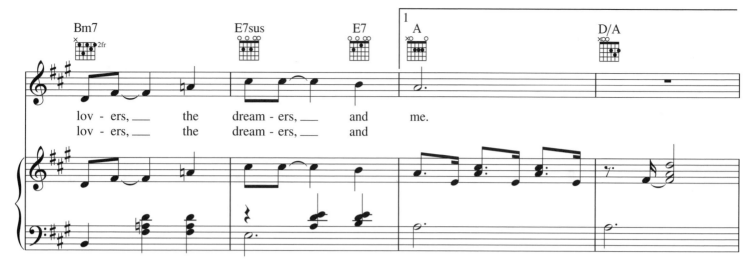

lov - ers, ___ the dream - ers, ___ and me.
lov - ers, ___ the dream - ers, ___ and

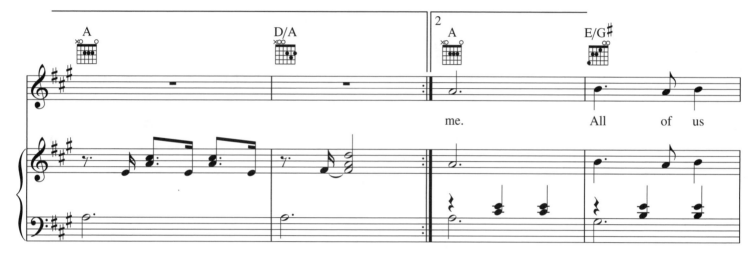

me. All of us

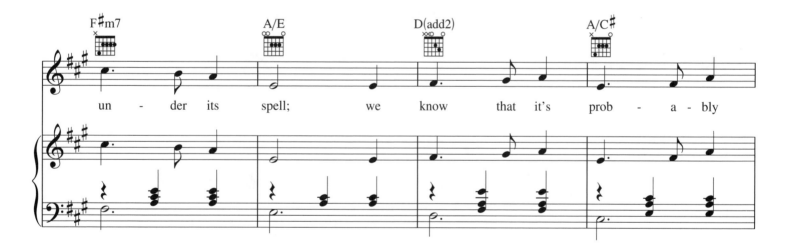

un - der its spell; we know that it's prob - a - bly

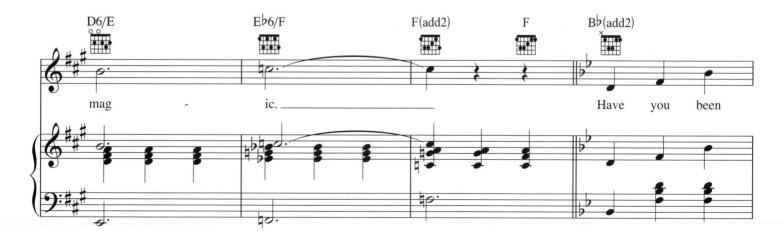

mag - ic. _____ Have you been

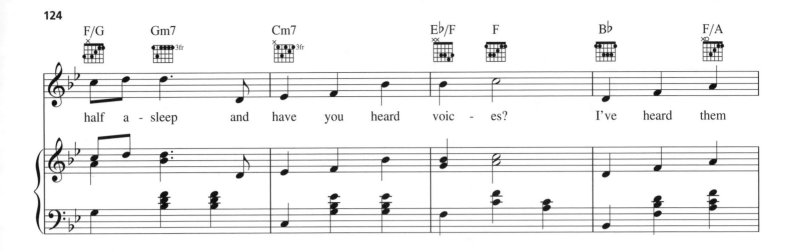

half a-sleep and have you heard voic - es? I've heard them

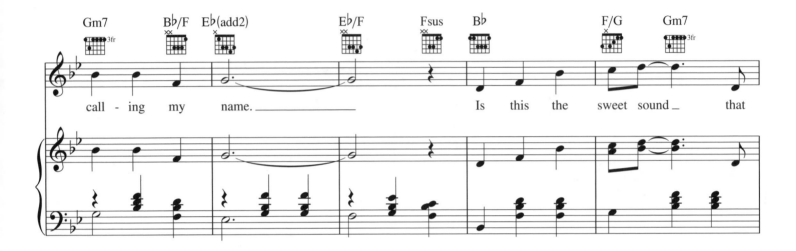

call - ing my name. _____ Is this the sweet sound _ that

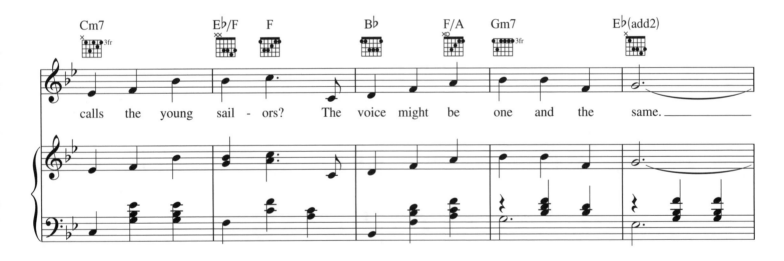

calls the young sail - ors? The voice might be one and the same. _____

_ I've heard it too man - y times to ig -

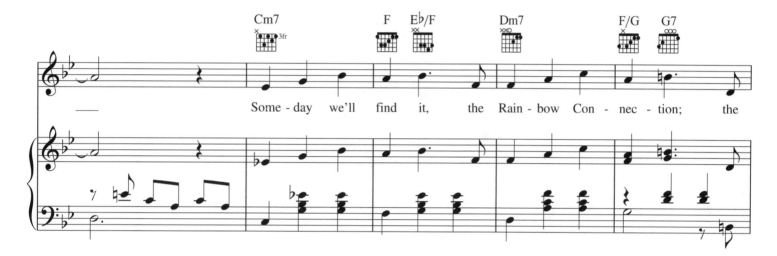

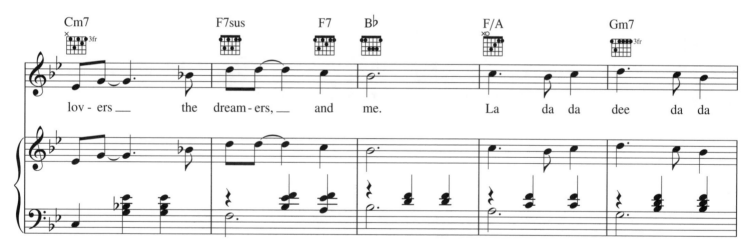

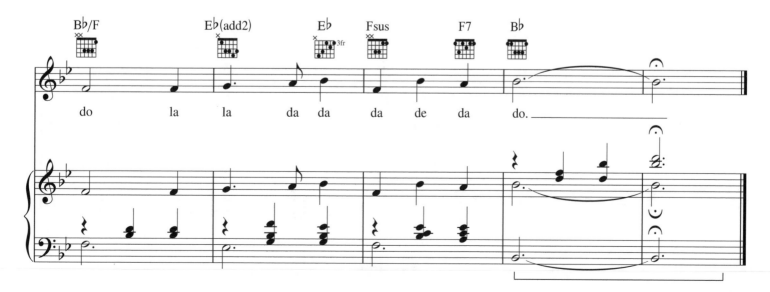

THE PETITE WALTZ

English Lyric by E.A. ELLINGTON and PHYLLIS CLAIRE
Music by JOE HEYNE

meant to be. _ Once a - gain we glide to ev - 'ry mag - ic strain,
mer - veil - leux. J'ai ou - vert ma mai - son A ta jo - lie chan - son,
rir sans fin. Lais - se moi m'en - vo - ler Vers d'au - tres fi - an - cés,

And I hold heav - en close with - in my arms a - gain. _ Tho' it's
Et j'ai ou - vert mon coeur A ton jo - li bon - heur. De - puis, sous
Of - frir aux a - mou - reux Des re - frains blancs et bleus. Pa - reil - le

just a dream, a bit of bit - ter sweet, _ It's our mel - o - dy.
no - tre toît, Nous vi - vons tous les trois, La val - se, toi et moi,
à une fée, Je ne fais que pas - ser, Al - lant de coeur en coeur

a waltz pe - tite. _ tite. _
I - vres de joie. _
Por - ter bon - heur. _

128

toast, A toast to the ghost of your last kiss._____
rait Ja - mais s'en al - ler Si tu res - tais._____
rait

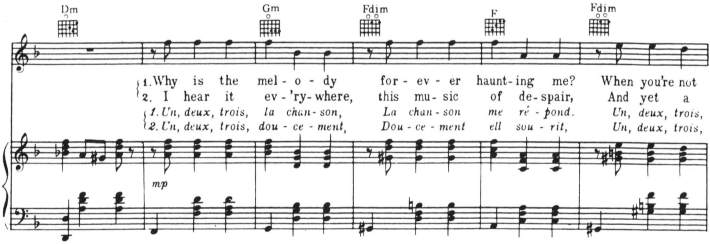

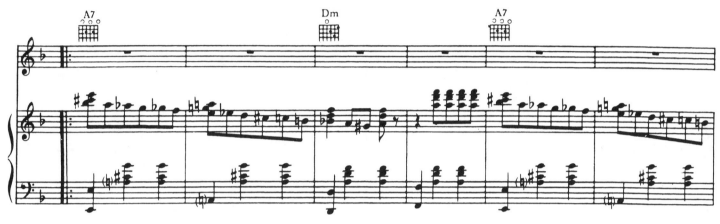

1.Why is the mel - o - dy for - ev - er haunt-ing me? When you're not
2. I hear it ev-'ry-where, this mu - sic of de-spair, And yet a
1.Un, deux, trois, la chan-son, La chan - son me ré - pond. Un, deux, trois,
2.Un, deux, trois, dou - ce - ment, Dou-ce - ment ell sou - rit, Un, deux, trois,

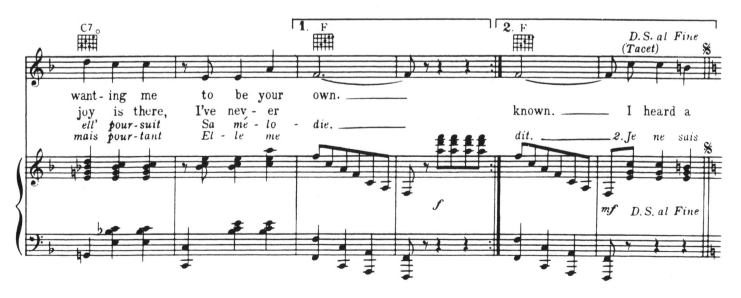

want-ing me to be your own._____
joy is there, I've nev - er known._____ I heard a
ell' pour-suit Sa mé - lo - die._____
mais pour-tant El - le me dit._____ 2.Je ne sais

D.S. al Fine
(Tacet)

QUE SERA, SERA
(Whatever Will Be, Will Be)
from THE MAN WHO KNEW TOO MUCH

Words and Music by JAY LIVINGSTON
and RAY EVANS

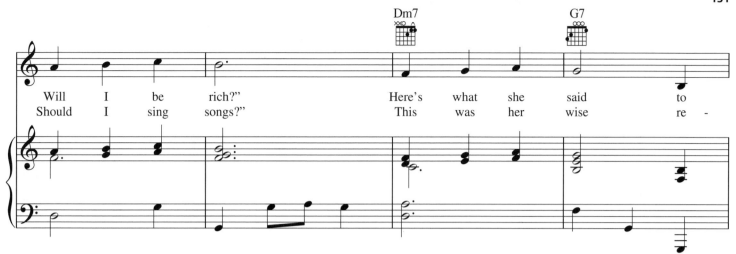

Will I be rich?" / Should I sing songs?"
Here's what she said to / This was her wise re-

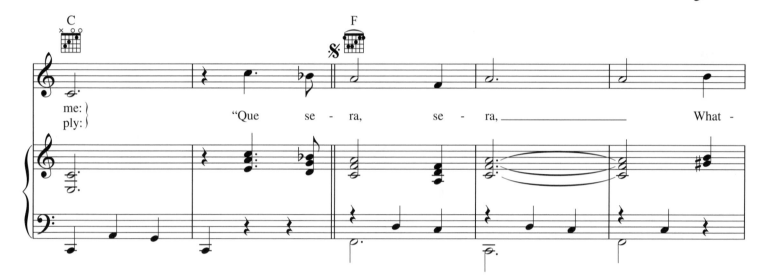

me: / ply:
"Que se - ra, se - ra, _____ What-

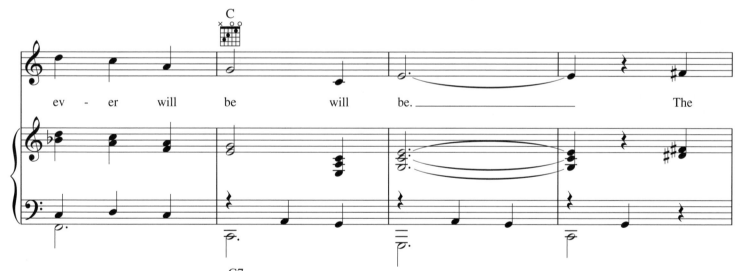

ev - er will be will be. _____ The

fu - ture's not ours to see. Que se -

THE SWEETHEART OF SIGMA CHI

Words by BYRON D. STOKES
Music by F. DUDLEIGH VERNOR

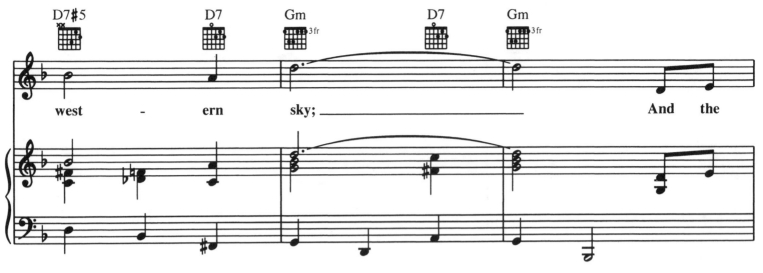

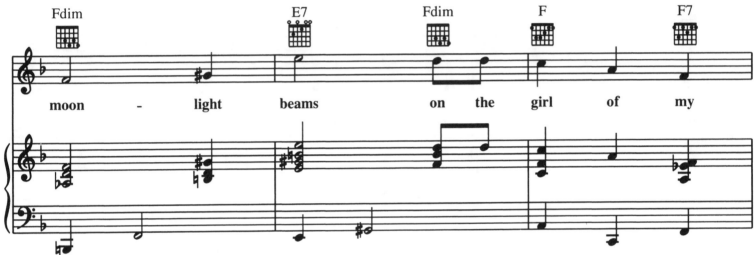

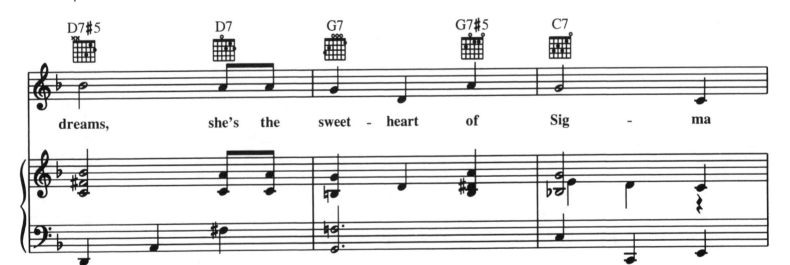

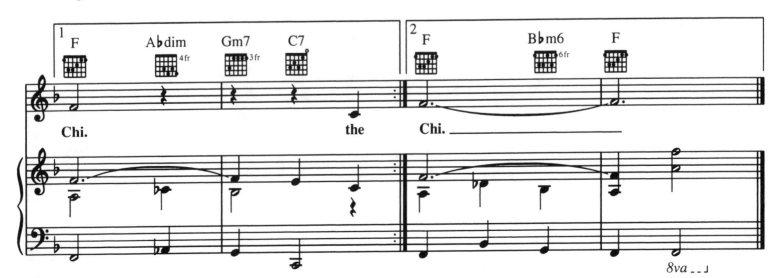

8va

TENDERLY
from TORCH SONG

Lyric by JACK LAWRENCE
Music by WALTER GROSS

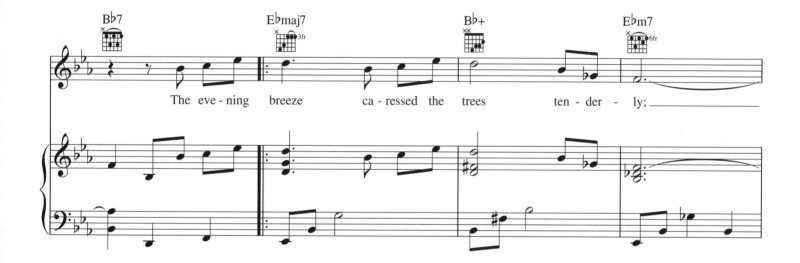

The eve-ning breeze ca-ressed the trees ten-der - ly; ____

____ the trem-bling trees em-braced the breeze ten-der - ly. ____

138

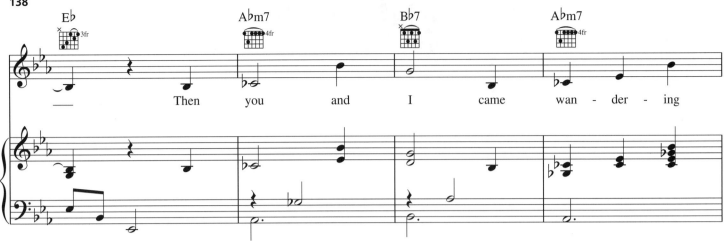

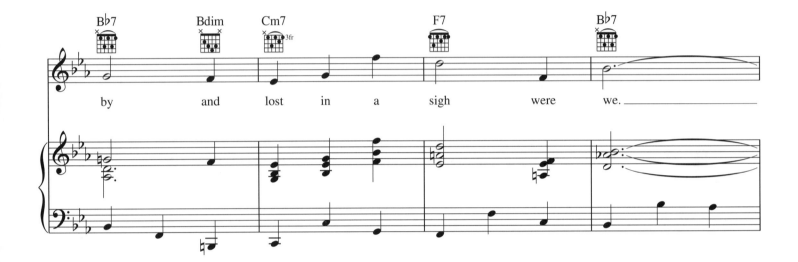

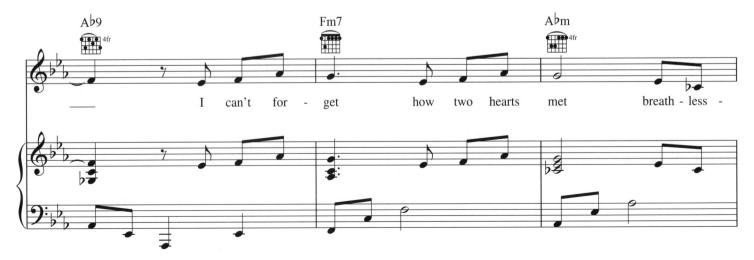

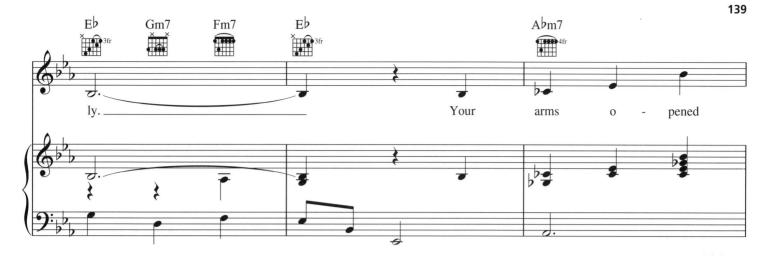

ly. _____ Your arms o - pened

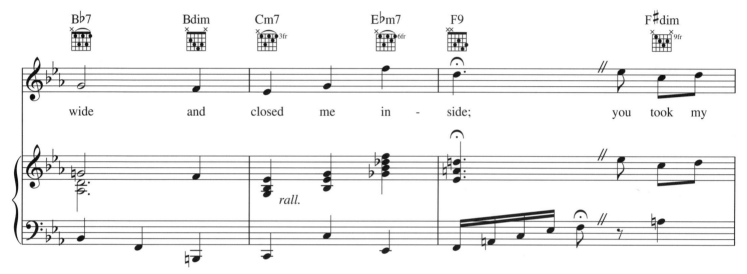

wide   and   closed   me   in - side;   you   took   my

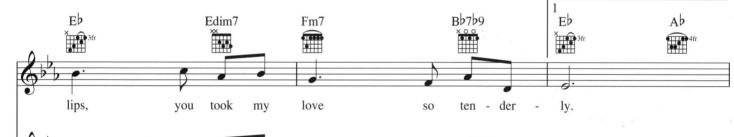

lips,   you   took   my   love   so   ten - der - ly.

The   eve - ning   ly. _____

TAMMY
from TAMMY AND THE BACHELOR

Words and Music by
JAY LIVINGSTON and RAY EVANS

TENNESSEE WALTZ

Words and Music by REDD STEWART
and PEE WEE KING

duced him to my loved one and ___ while they were ___

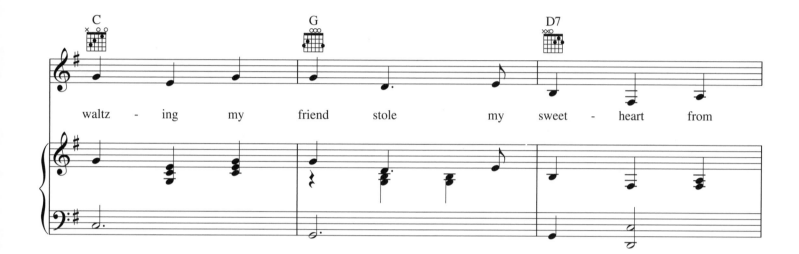

waltz - ing my friend stole my sweet - heart from

me. _____ I re - mem - ber the night and the

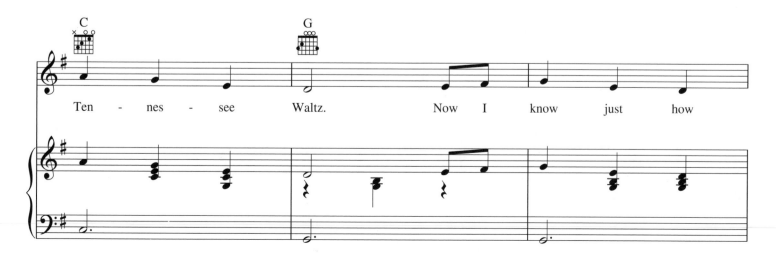

Ten - nes - see Waltz. Now I know just how

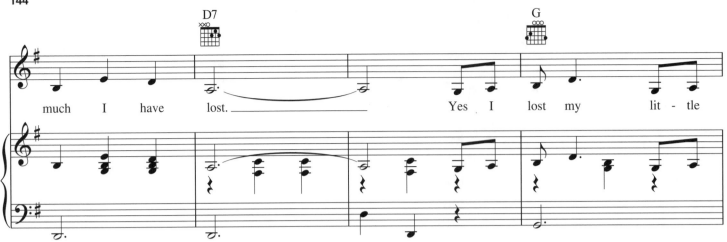

much I have lost. _____ Yes I lost my lit - tle

dar - lin' the ___ night they were ___ play - ing the

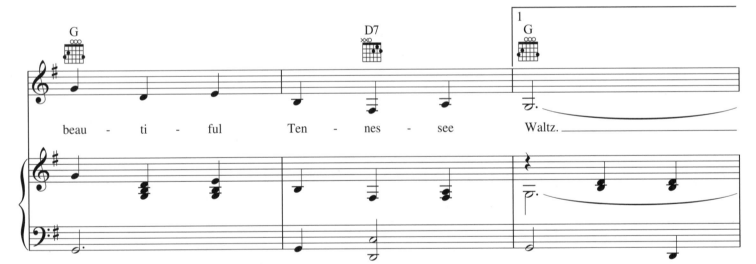

beau - ti - ful Ten - nes - see Waltz. _____

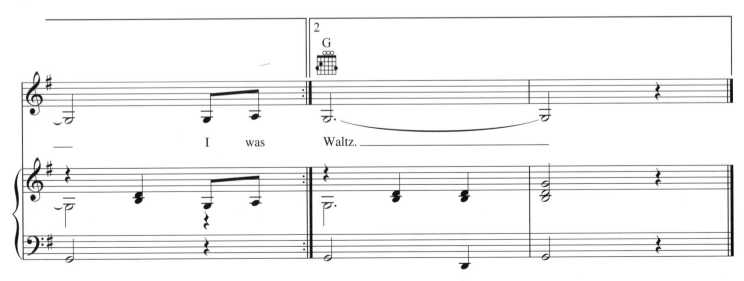

I was Waltz. _____

THAT'S AMORÉ
(That's Love)
from the Paramount Picture THE CADDY

Words by JACK BROOKS
Music by HARRY WARREN

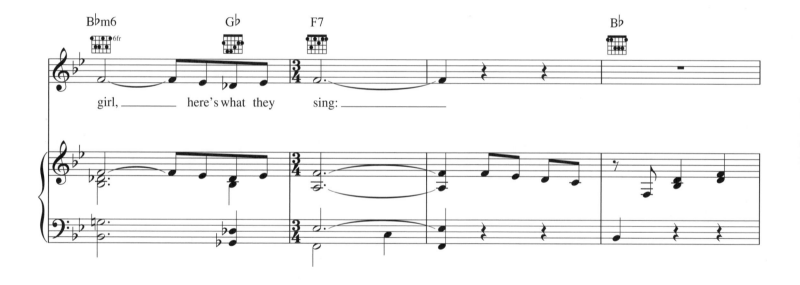

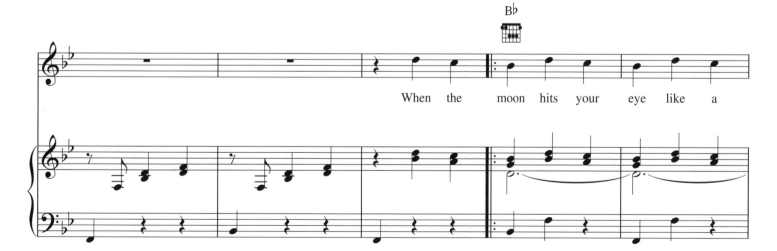

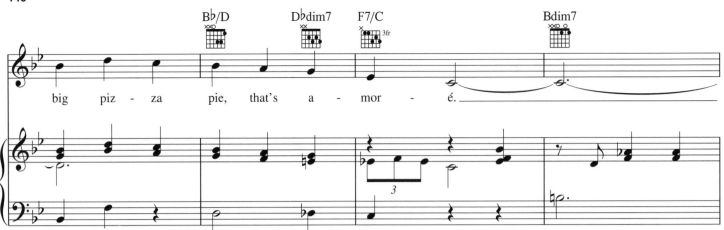

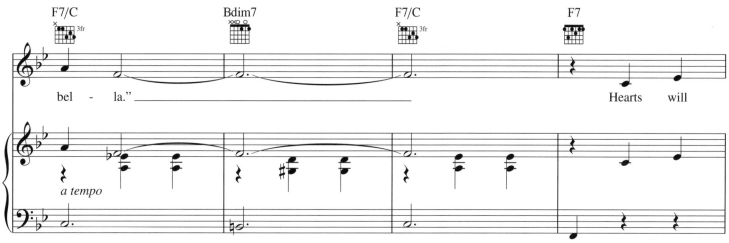

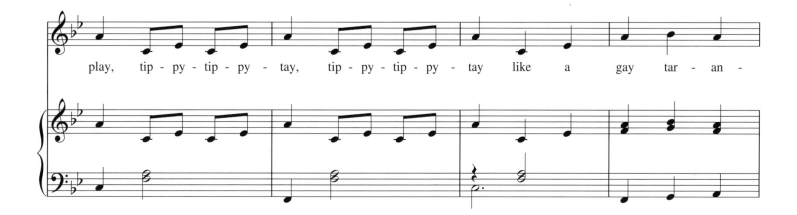

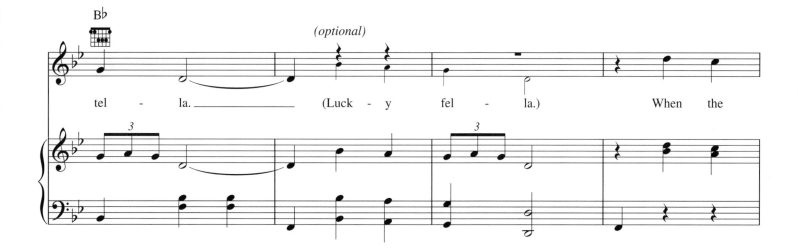

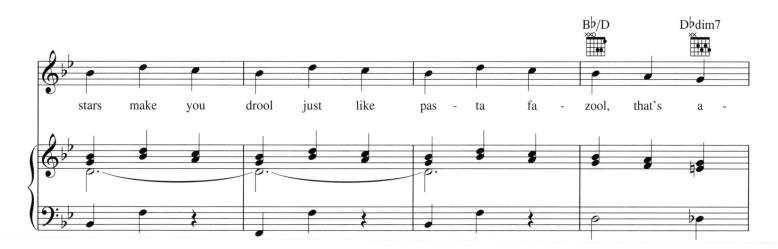

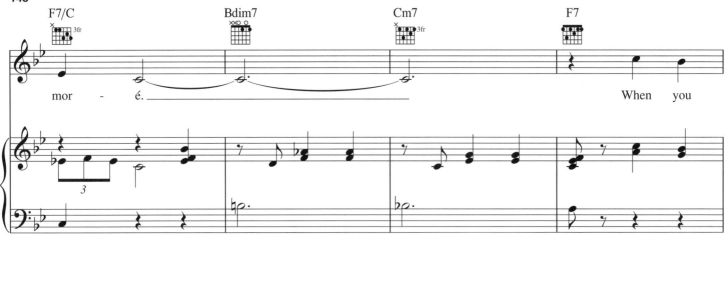

mor - é. When you

dance down the street with a cloud at your feet, you're in

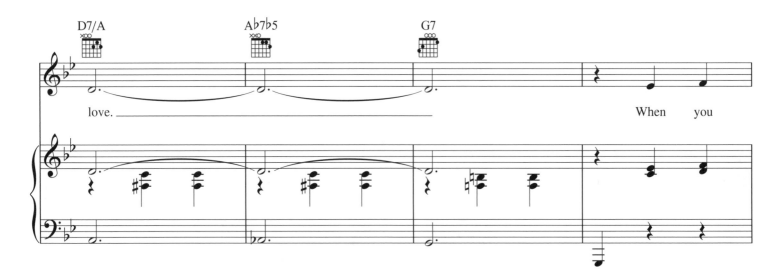

love. When you

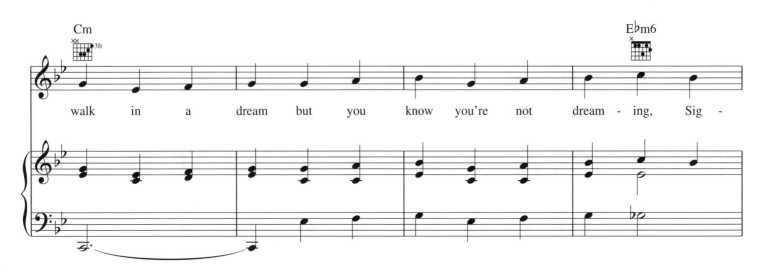

walk in a dream but you know you're not dream-ing, Sig -

nor - é, _____ scuz - za

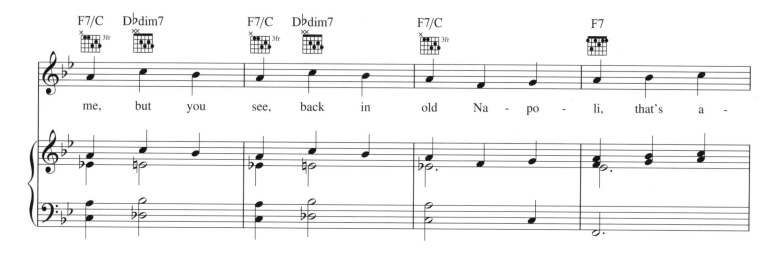

me, but you see, back in old Na - po - li, that's a -

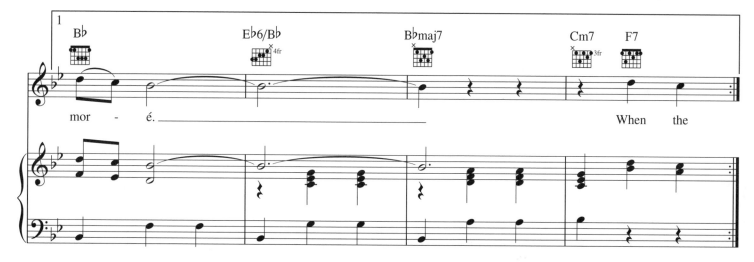

mor - é. _____ When the

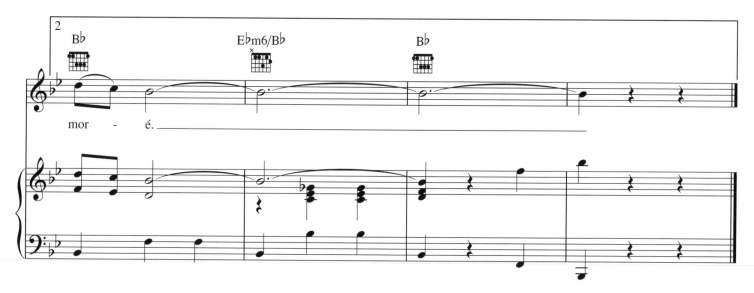

mor - é. _____

THIS NEARLY WAS MINE

from SOUTH PACIFIC

Lyrics by OSCAR HAMMERSTEIN II
Music by RICHARD RODGERS

Verse

So clear and deep are my fan - cies

Of things I wish were true. I'll

keep re - mem - b'ring eve - nings I wish I'd

spent with you. I'll keep re -

A TIME FOR US
(Love Theme)
from the Paramount Picture ROMEO AND JULIET

Words by LARRY KUSIK and EDDIE SNYDER
Music by NINO ROTA

nied _____ can flour - ish _____ as we un - veil the

love we now must hide. _____ A time _____ for us _____ at

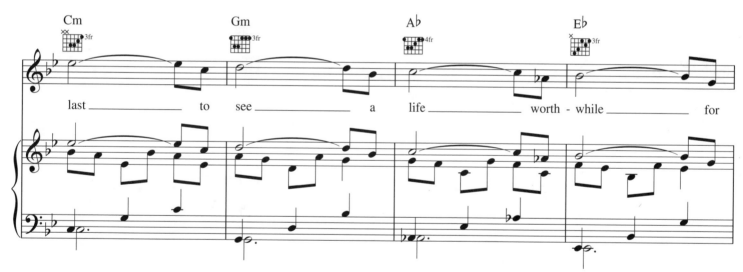

last _____ to see _____ a life _____ worth - while _____ for

you _____ and me. And with our love through tears and

TRUE LOVE
from HIGH SOCIETY

Words and Music by
COLE PORTER

Moderately slow

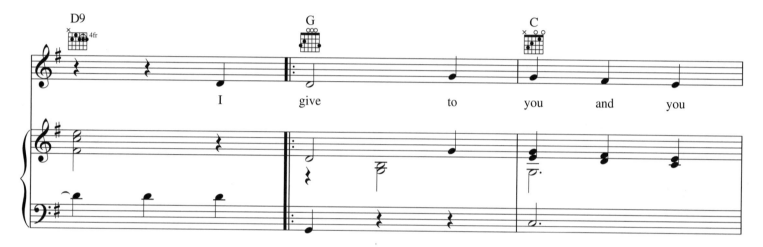

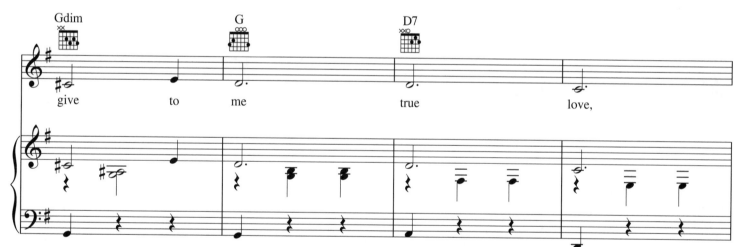

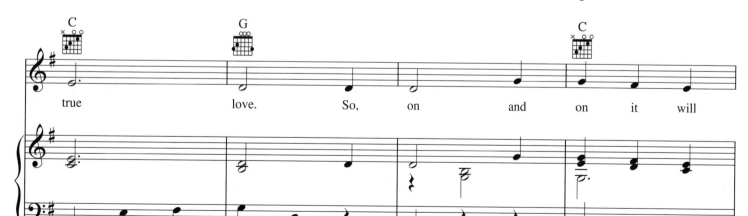

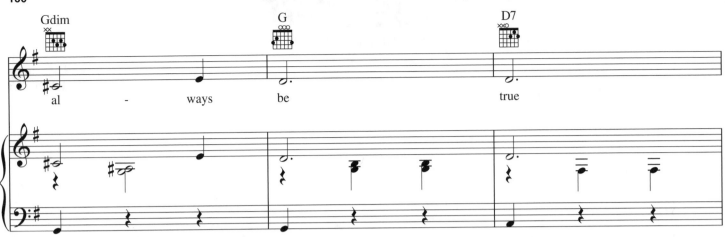

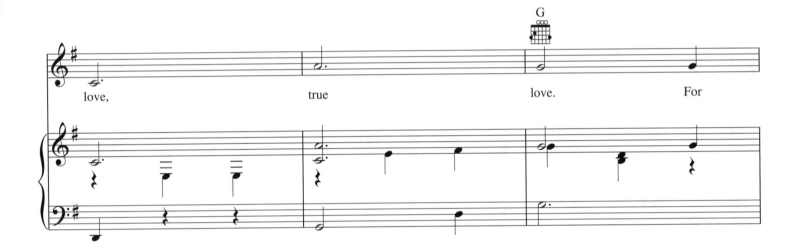

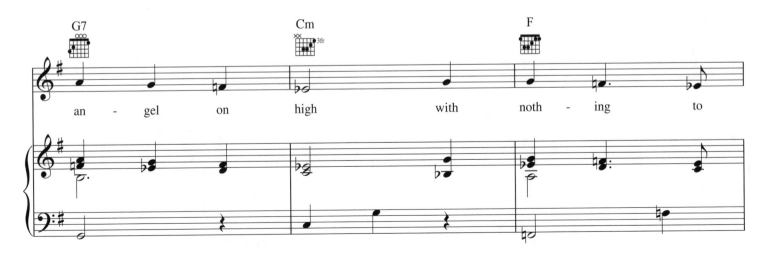

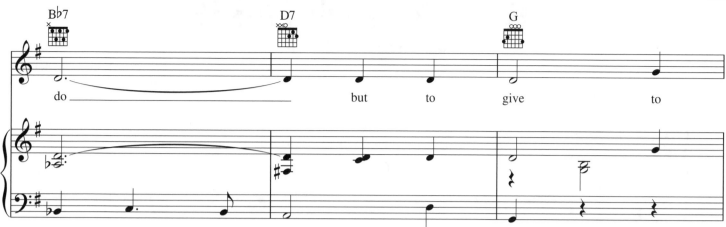

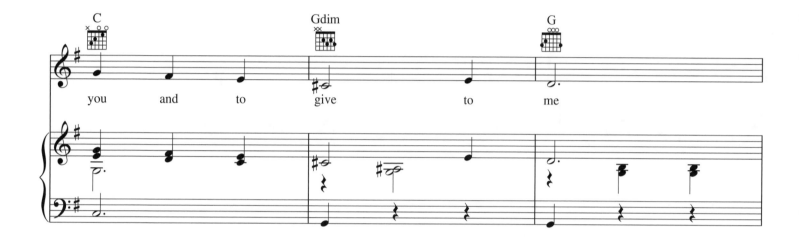

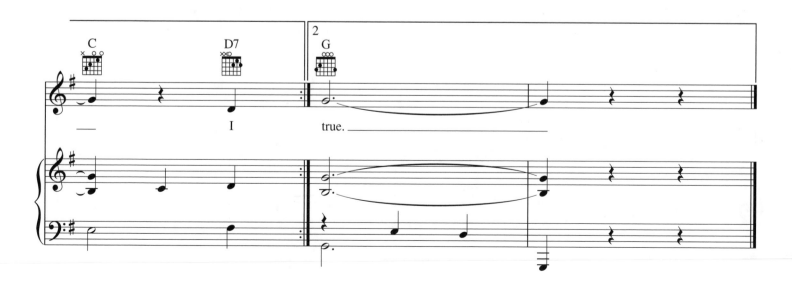

TRY TO REMEMBER

from THE FANTASTICKS

Words by TOM JONES
Music by HARVEY SCHMIDT

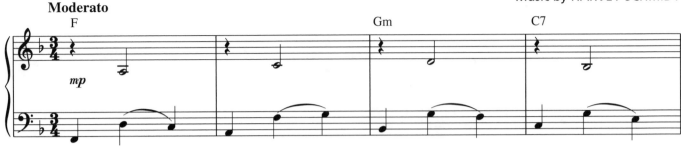

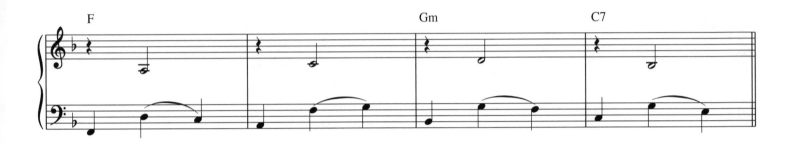

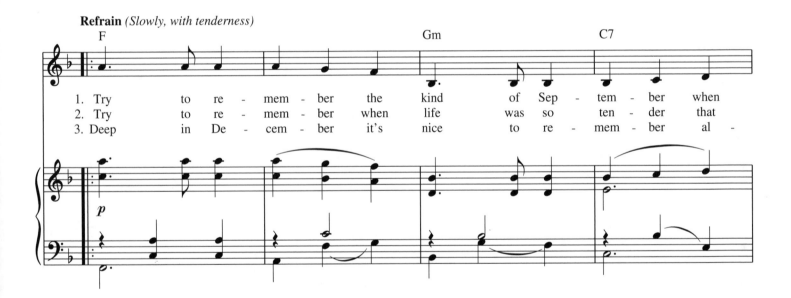

1. Try to re-mem-ber the kind of Sep-tem-ber when
2. Try to re-mem-ber when life was so ten-der that
3. Deep in De-cem-ber it's nice to re-mem-ber al -

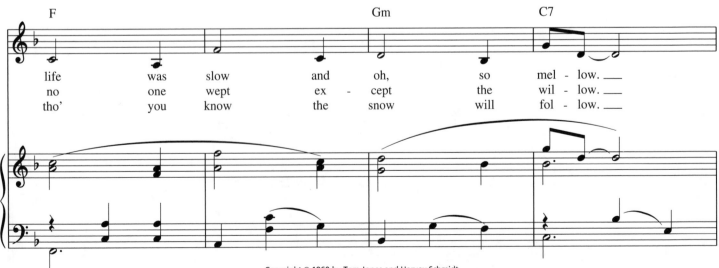

life was slow and oh, so mel - low. __
no one wept ex - cept the wil - low. __
tho' you know the snow will fol - low. __

Try to re - mem - ber and if you re - mem - ber, then
Try to re - mem - ber and if you re - mem - ber, then
Deep in De - cem - ber our hearts should re - mem - ber and

fol - low. ____
fol - low. ____

fol - low. ____

fol - low. _____

rit. e decresc.

WHAT THE WORLD NEEDS NOW IS LOVE

Lyric by HAL DAVID
Music by BURT BACHARACH

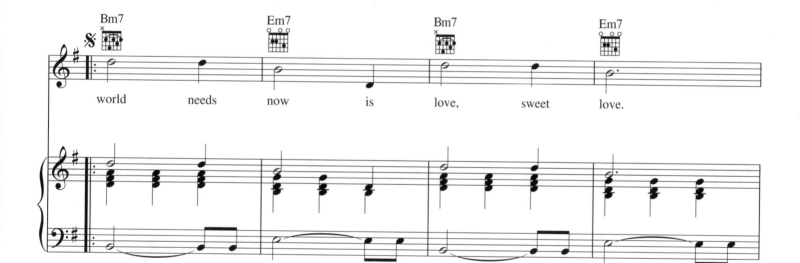

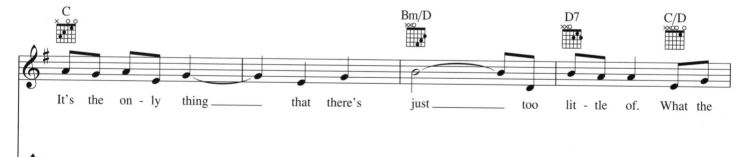

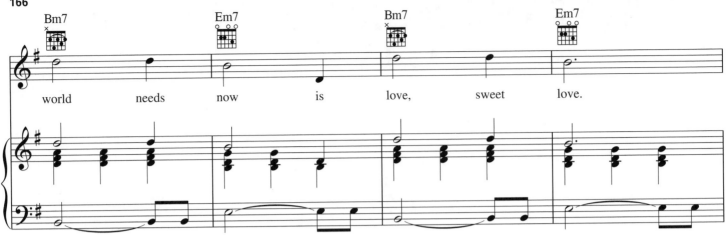

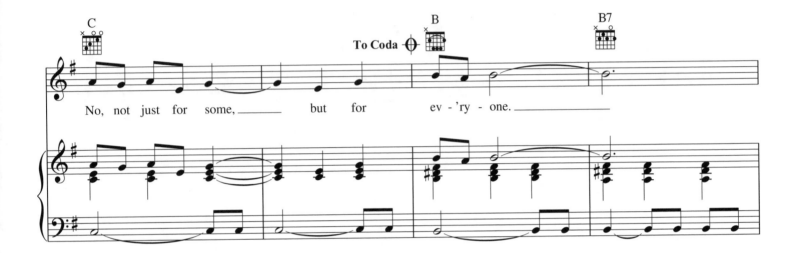

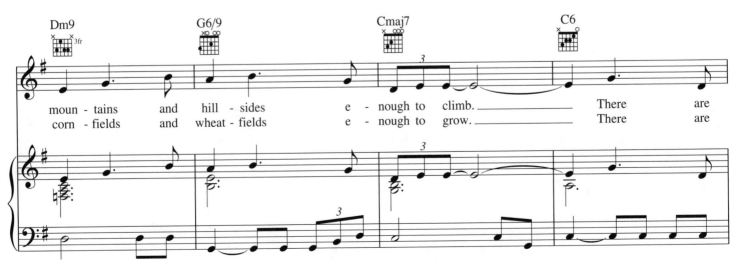

o - ceans and riv - ers e - nough to cross,_____ e - nough to last __
sun - beams and moon - beams e - nough to shine,_____ oh, lis - ten, Lord, _

till the end of time._____ What the
if you want to know._____ What the

ev - 'ry - one. _____ No, not just for some,_____ oh, but

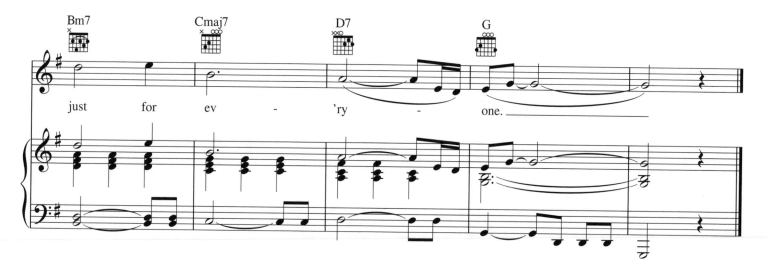

just for ev - 'ry - one. _____

WHAT'LL I DO?

from MUSIC BOX REVUE OF 1924

Words and Music by
IRVING BERLIN

Gone is the ro - mance that was so di - vine.
Do you re - mem - ber that a night was so filled with bliss?

'Tis bro - ken and can - not be mend - ed.
The moon - light was soft - ly de - scend - ing.

You must go
Your lips and

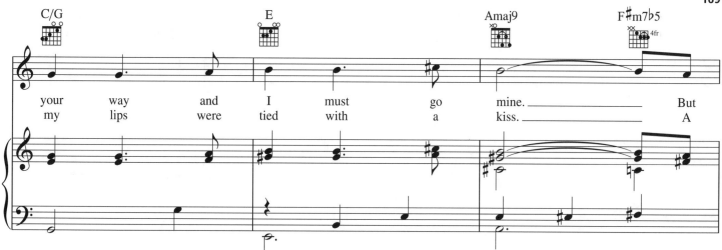

your way and I must go mine. _____ But
my lips were tied with a kiss. _____ A

now that our love dreams have end -
kiss with an un - hap - py end -

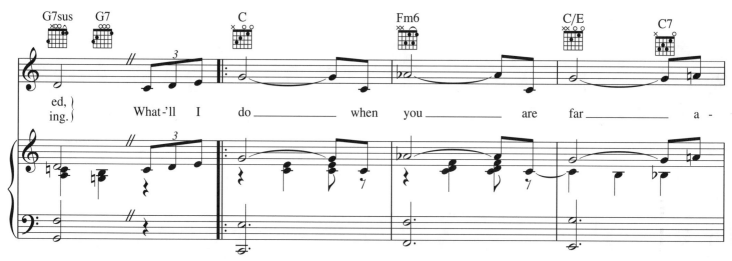

ed, }
ing. } What -'ll I do _____ when you _____ are far _____ a -

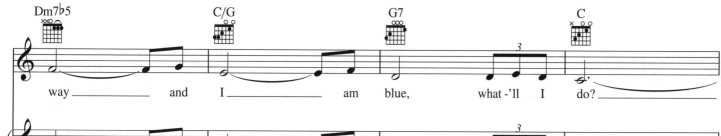

way _____ and I _____ am blue, what -'ll I do? _____

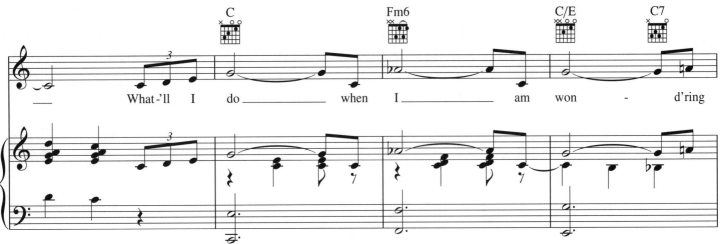

What-'ll I do _____ when I _____ am won - d'ring

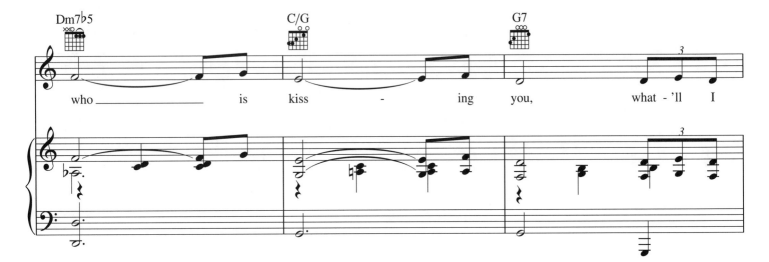

who _____ is kiss - ing you, what-'ll I

do? _____ What-'ll I do _____ with

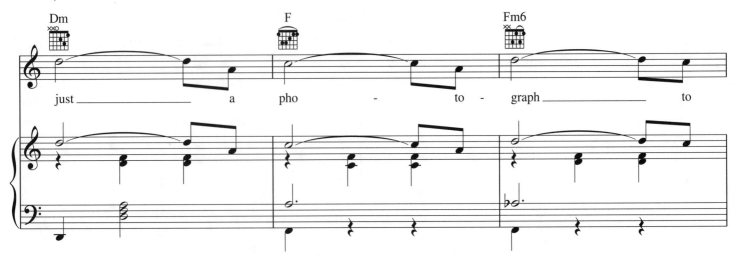

just _____ a pho - to - graph _____ to

WHEN I'M NOT NEAR THE GIRL I LOVE

from FINIAN'S RAINBOW

Words by E.Y. HARBURG
Music by BURTON LANE

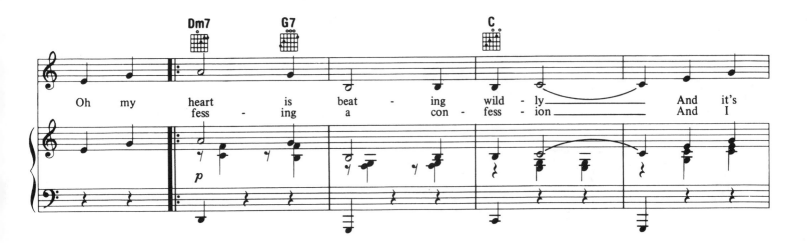

Oh my heart is beat-ing wild-ly ___ And it's
fess - ing a con- fess - ion ___ And I

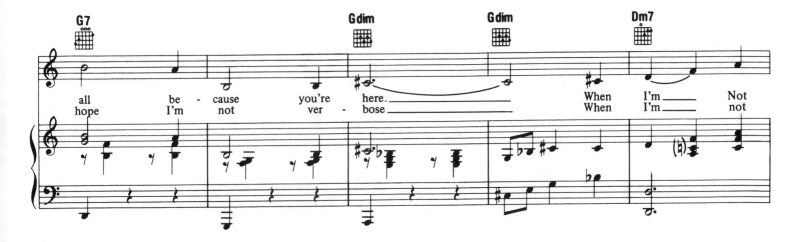

all be - cause you're here. ___ When I'm ___ Not
hope I'm not ver - bose ___ When I'm ___ not

WUNDERBAR
from KISS ME, KATE

Words and Music by
COLE PORTER

Tempo di Valse (*lively*)

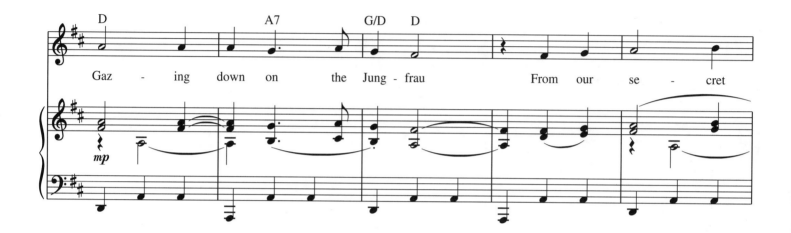

Gaz - ing down on the Jung - frau From our se - cret

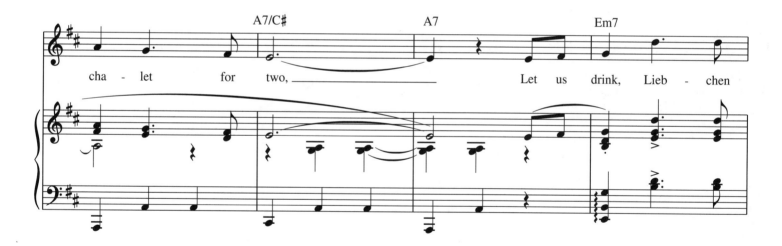

cha - let for two, _____ Let us drink, Lieb - chen

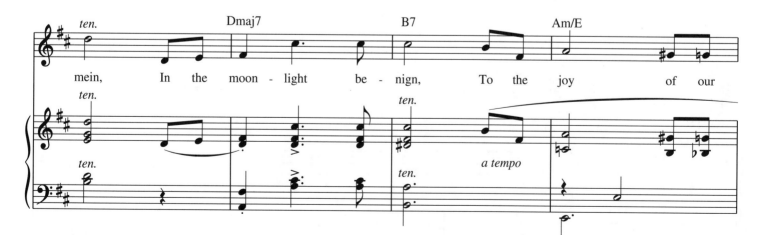

mein, In the moon - light be - nign, To the joy of our

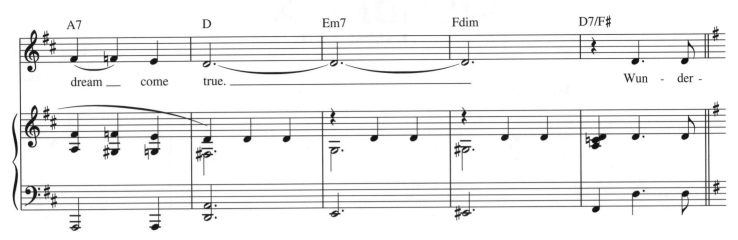

176

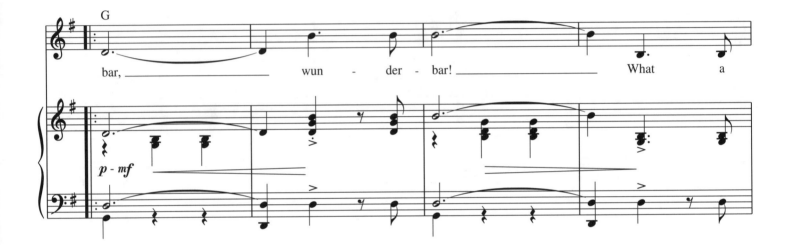

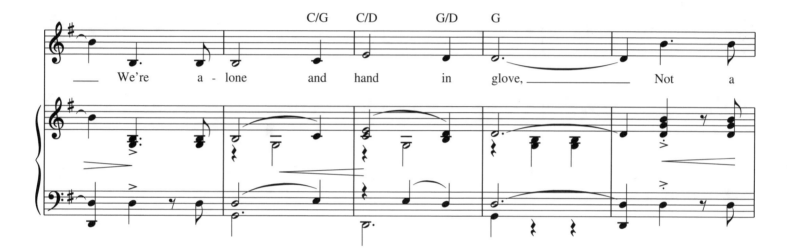

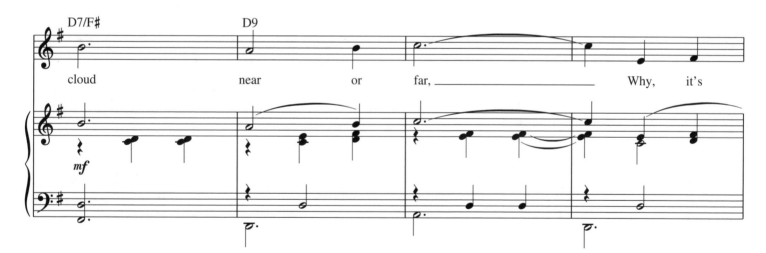

C/G C/D G/D

bar!_____ There's our fav'-rite star a - bove,_____

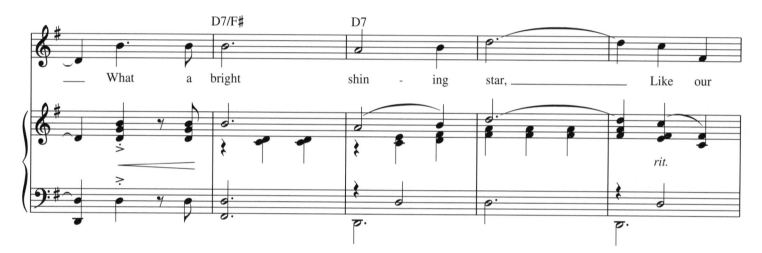

D7/F♯   D7

____ What a bright shin - ing star,_____ Like our

1
Gsus   G   D7

love, it's wun - der - bar!_____ Wun - der -

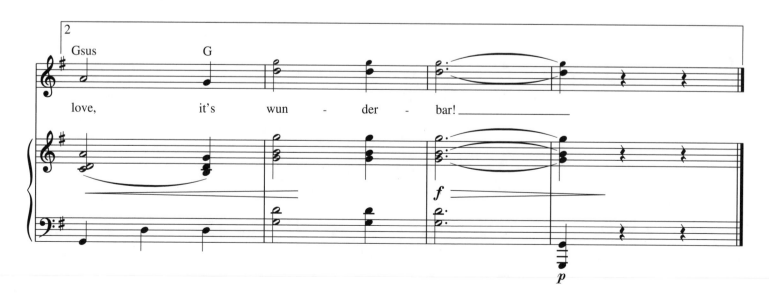

2
Gsus   G

love, it's wun - der - bar!_____

f

p

IRISH EYES ARE SMILING

Words by CHAUNCEY OLCOTT
and GEORGE GRAFF, JR.
Music by ERNEST R. BALL

179

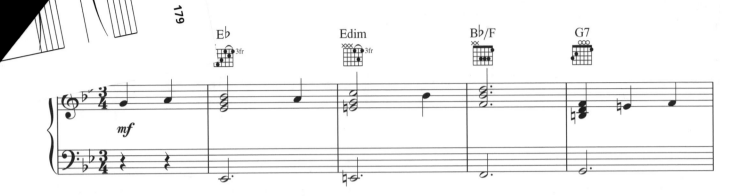

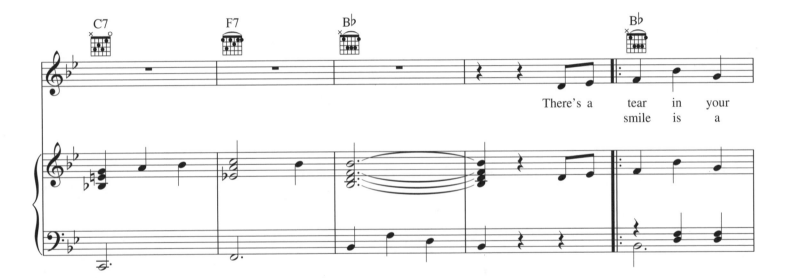

There's a tear in your
smile is a

eye, and I'm won-der-ing why, for it nev-er should be there at
part of the love in your heart, and it makes e-ven sun-shine more

all. _____ With such pow'r in your smile, sure a stone you'd be-

bright. _____ Like the lin-net's sweet song, croon-ing all the day

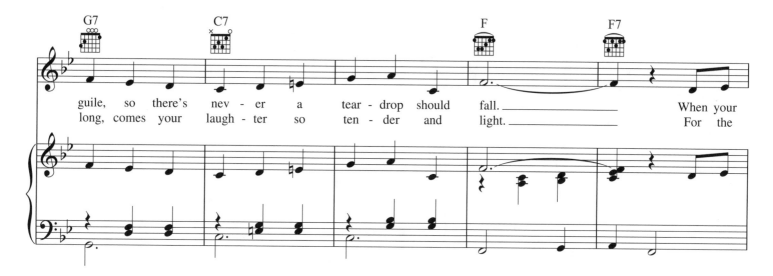

guile, so there's nev-er a tear-drop should fall. _____ When your

long, comes your laugh-ter so ten-der and light. _____ For the

sweet lilt-ing laugh-ter's like some fair-y song, and your eyes twin-kle

spring-time of life is the sweet-est of all, there is ne'er a real

bright as can be, _____ you should laugh all the while and all

care or re-gret. _____ And while spring-time is ours through-out

oth - er times, while, and now smile ___ a smile for me. ___
all of youth's hours, let us smile ___ each chance we get. ___

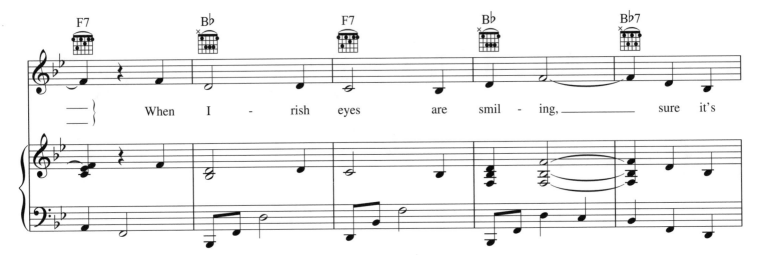

___ } When I - rish eyes are smil - ing, ___ sure it's

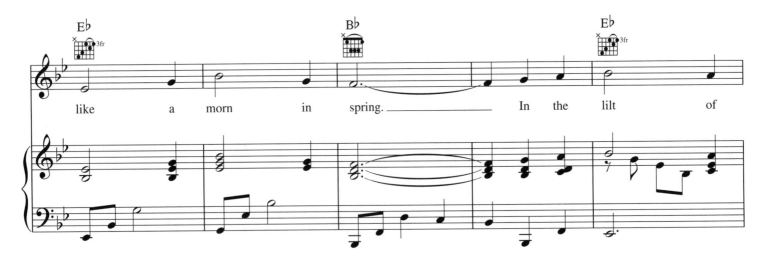

like a morn in spring. ___ In the lilt of

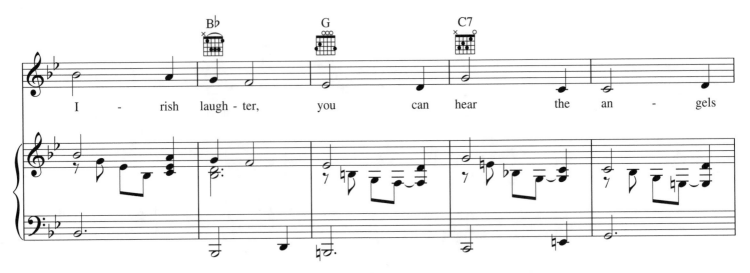

I - rish laugh - ter, you can hear the an - gels

sing. _____ When I - rish hearts are hap - py, _____

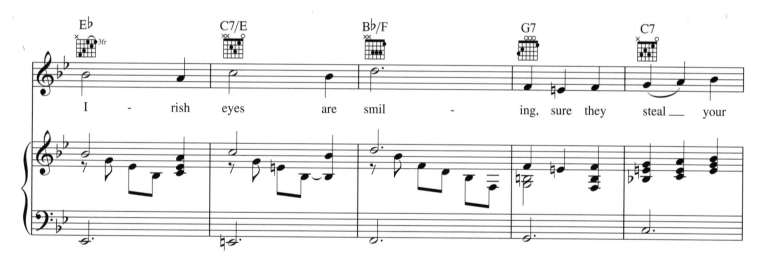

____ all the world seems bright and gay. _____ And when

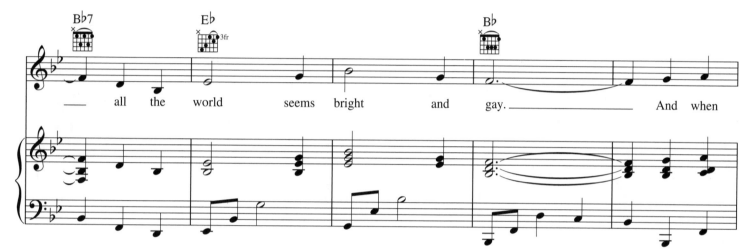

I - rish eyes are smil - ing, sure they steal ___ your

heart a - way. _____ For your way.

WIVES AND LOVERS
(Hey, Little Girl)
from the Paramount Picture WIVES AND LOVERS

Words by HAL DAVID
Music by BURT BACHARACH

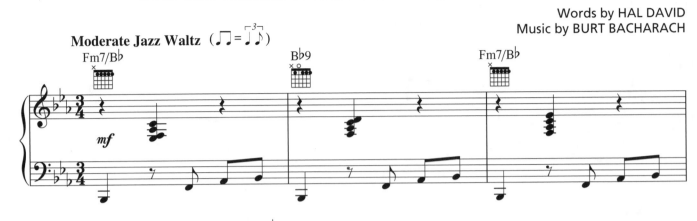

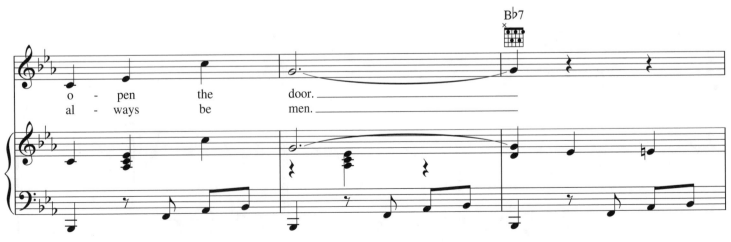

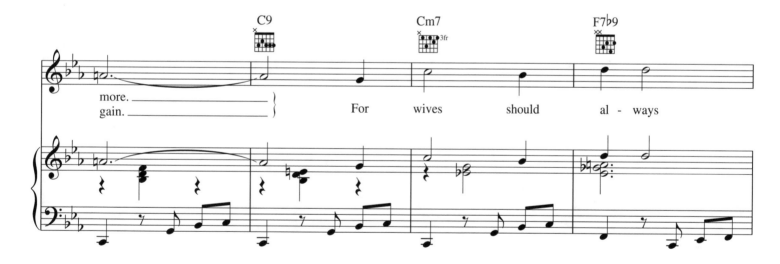

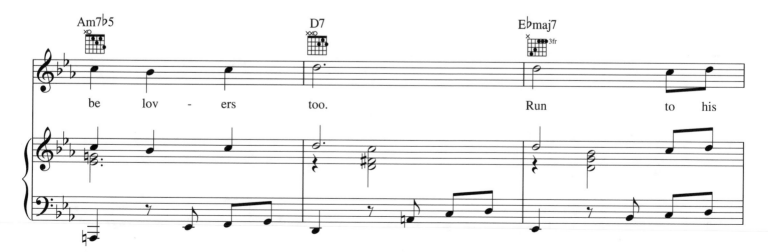

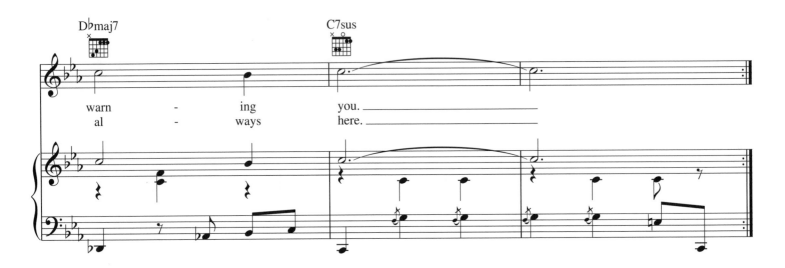

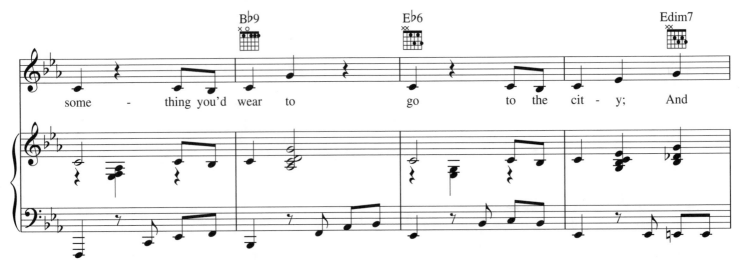

dim all the lights, pour the wine, start the mu - sic,

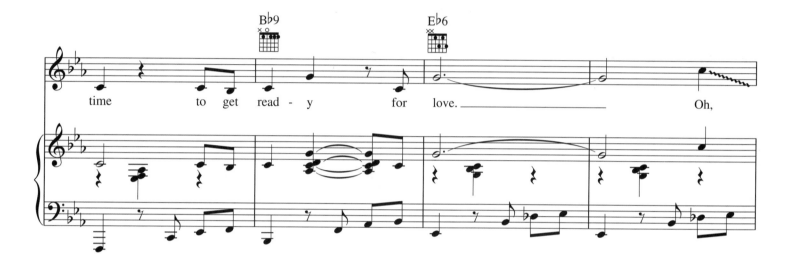

time to get read - y for love. _____ Oh,

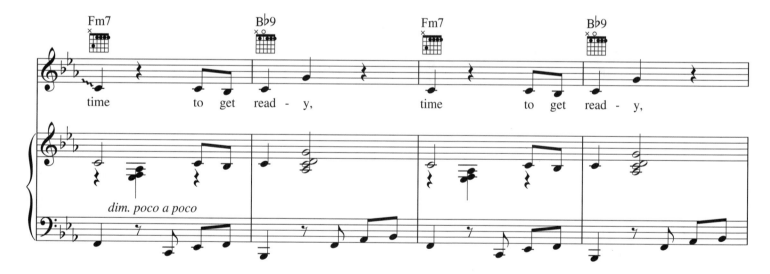

time to get read - y, time to get read - y,

dim. poco a poco

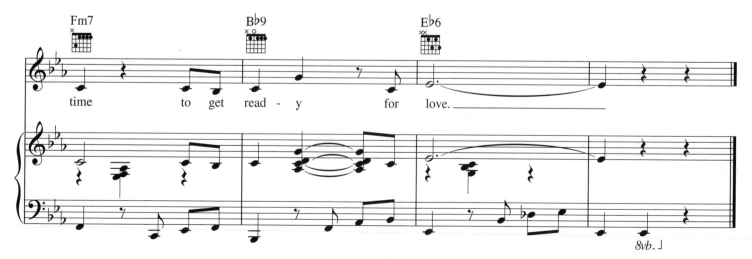

time to get read - y for love. _____

8vb

A WONDERFUL GUY

from SOUTH PACIFIC

Lyrics by OSCAR HAMMERSTEIN II
Music by RICHARD RODGERS

Allegro moderato

I ex-

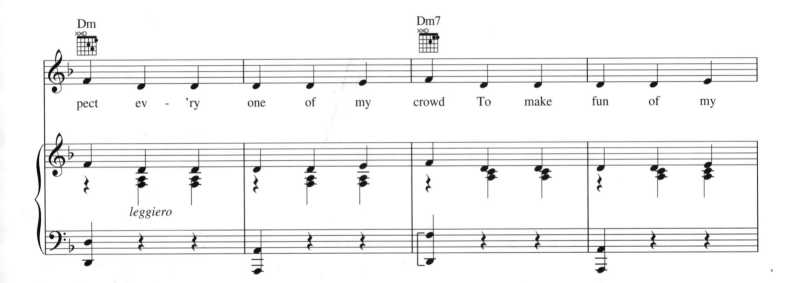

pect ev - 'ry one of my crowd To make fun of my

proud pro - tes - ta - tions Of faith in ro - mance.

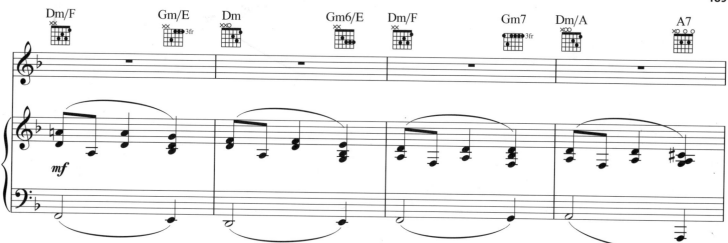

And they'll

say I'm na - ive As a babe to be - lieve An - y

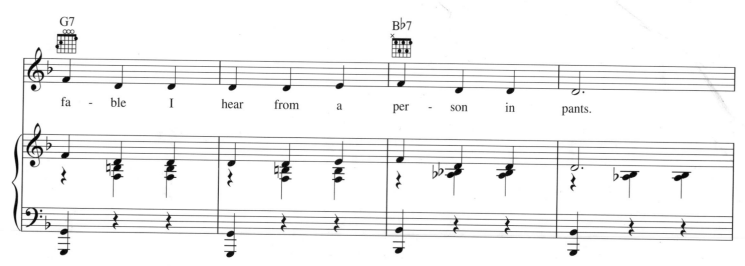

fa - ble I hear from a per - son in pants.

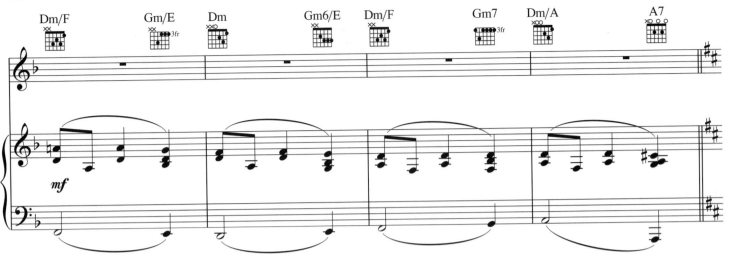

Fear - less - ly I'll face them and ar - gue their

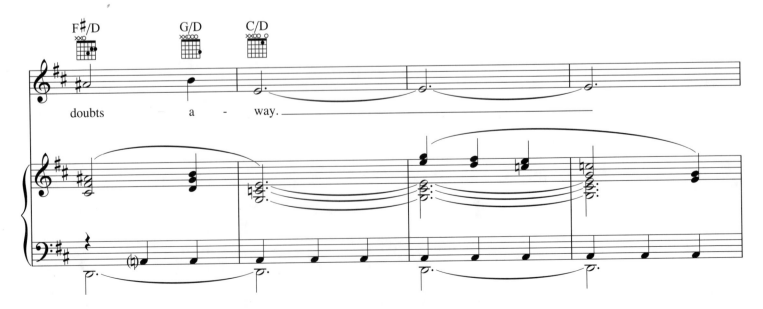

doubts a - way. _____

world   fa - mous   feel - ing   I

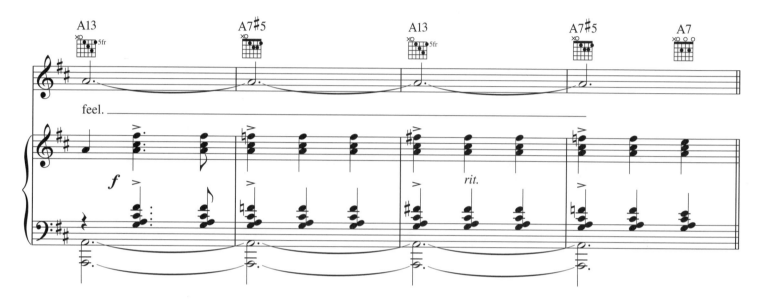

feel. _____

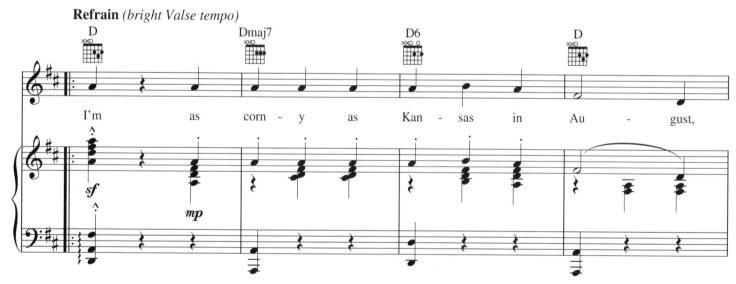

Refrain *(bright Valse tempo)*

I'm   as   corn - y   as   Kan - sas   in   Au - gust,

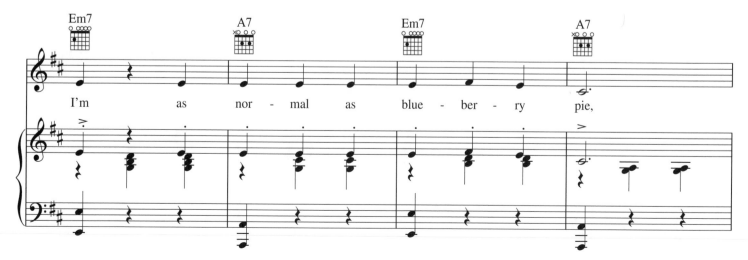

I'm   as   nor - mal   as   blue - ber - ry   pie,

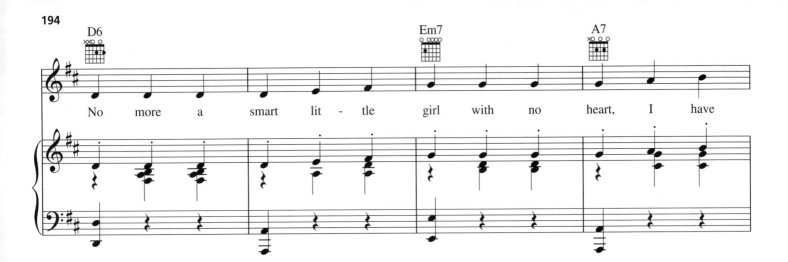

No more a smart lit-tle girl with no heart, I have

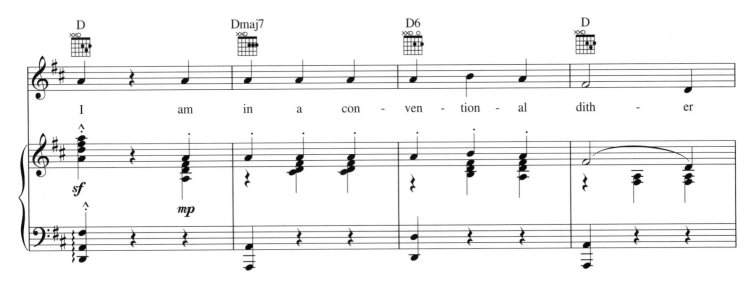

found me a won-der-ful guy! _____

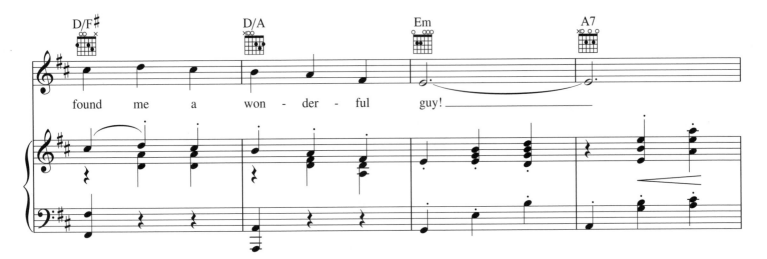

I am in a con-ven-tion-al dith - er

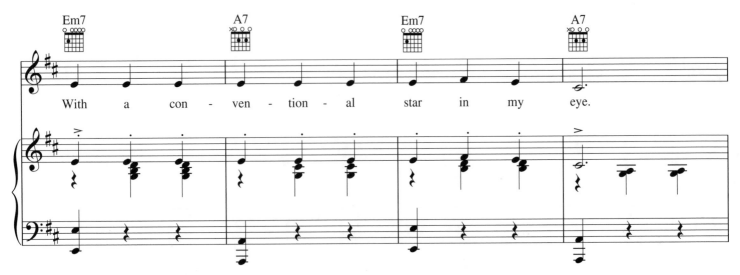

With a con-ven-tion-al star in my eye.

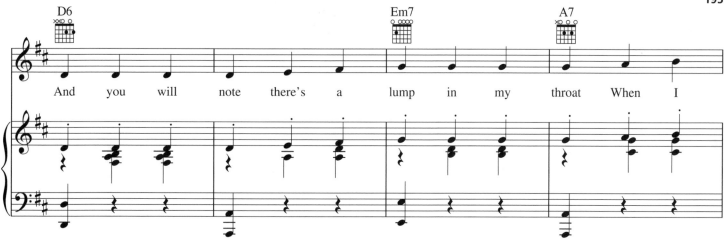

And you will note there's a lump in my throat When I

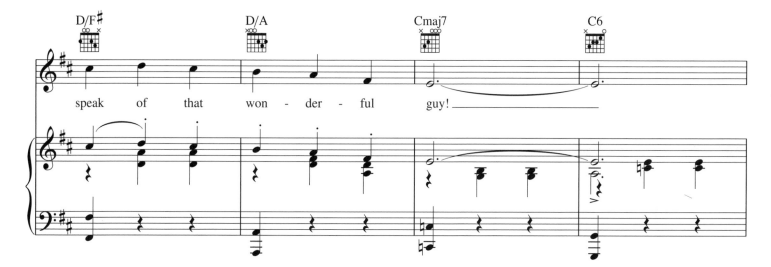

speak of that won-der-ful guy! _____

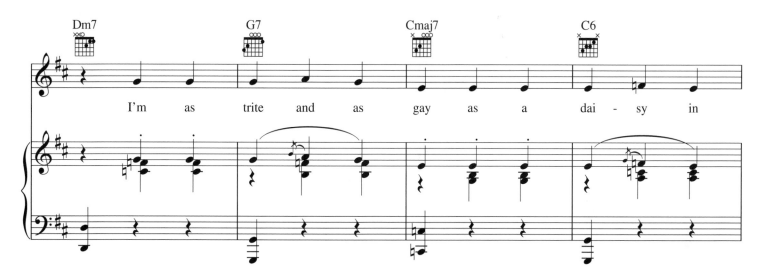

I'm as trite and as gay as a dai-sy in

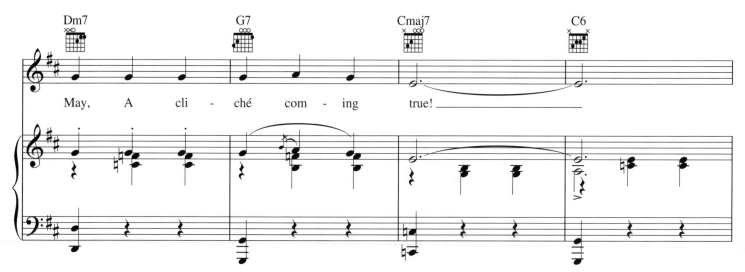

May, A cli-ché com-ing true! _____

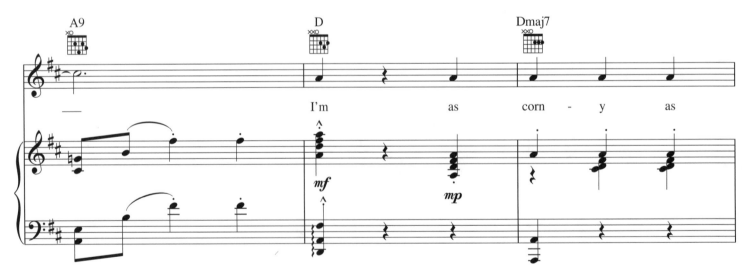

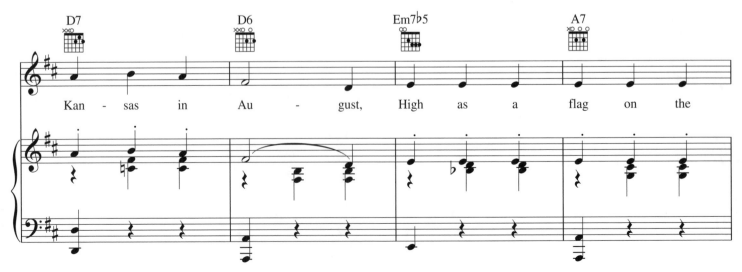

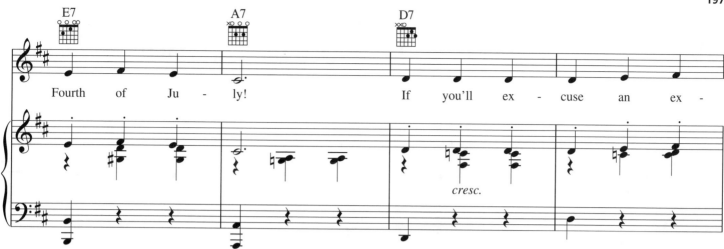

Fourth of Ju - ly! If you'll ex - cuse an ex -

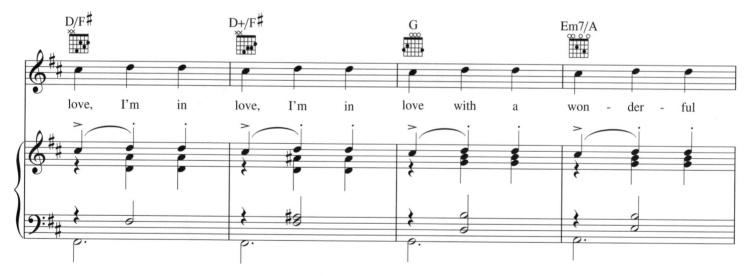

pres - sion I use, I'm in love, I'm in love, I'm in

love, I'm in love, I'm in love with a won - der - ful

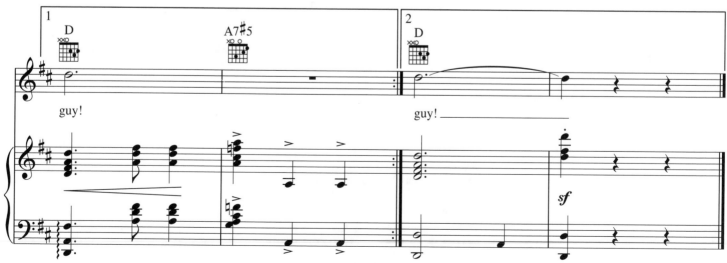

guy!

guy! _____

Classic Collections Of Your Favorite Songs

arranged for piano, voice, and guitar.

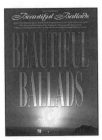

Beautiful Ballads

A massive collection of 87 songs, including: April in Paris • Autumn in New York • Call Me Irresponsible • Cry Me a River • I Wish You Love • I'll Be Seeing You • If • Imagine • Isn't It Romantic? • It's Impossible (Somos Novios) • Mona Lisa • Moon River • People • The Way We Were • A Whole New World (Aladdin's Theme) • and more.

00311679 ....$17.95

Irving Berlin Anthology

A comprehensive collection of 61 timeless songs with a bio, song background notes, and photos. Songs include: Always • Blue Skies • Cheek to Cheek • God Bless America • Marie • Puttin' on the Ritz • Steppin' Out with My Baby • There's No Business Like Show Business • White Christmas • (I Wonder Why?) You're Just in Love • and more.

00312493 ....$22.95

The Big Book of Standards

86 classics essential to any music library, including: April in Paris • Autumn in New York • Blue Skies • Cheek to Cheek • Heart and Soul • I Left My Heart in San Francisco • In the Mood • Isn't It Romantic? • Mona Lisa • Moon River • The Nearness of You • Out of Nowhere • Spanish Eyes • Star Dust • Stella by Starlight • That Old Black Magic • They Say It's Wonderful • What Now My Love • and more.

00311667 ....$19.95

Broadway Deluxe

This exciting collection of 125 of Broadway's biggest show tunes is deluxe indeed! Includes such showstoppers as: Bewitched • Cabaret • Camelot • Day by Day • Hello Young Lovers • I Could Have Danced All Night • I've Grown Accustomed to Her Face • If Ever I Would Leave You • The Lady Is a Tramp • I Talk to the Trees • My Heart Belongs to Daddy • Oklahoma • September Song • Seventy Six Trombones • Try to Remember • and more!

00309245 ....$24.95

Classic Jazz Standards

56 jazz essentials: All the Things You Are • Don't Get Around Much Anymore • How Deep Is the Ocean • In the Wee Small Hours of the Morning • Polka Dots and Moonbeams • Satin Doll • Skylark • Tangerine • Tenderly • What's New? • and more.

00310310 ....$16.95

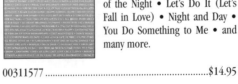

I'll Be Seeing You: 50 Songs of World War II

A salute to the music and memories of WWII, including a year-by-year chronology of events on the homefront, dozens of photos, and 50 radio favorites of the GIs and their families back home, including: Boogie Woogie Bugle Boy • Don't Sit Under the Apple Tree (With Anyone Else But Me) • I Don't Want to Walk Without You • I'll Be Seeing You • Moonlight in Vermont • There's a Star-Spangled Banner Waving Somewhere • You'd Be So Nice to Come Home To • and more.

00311698 ....$19.95

Lounge Music

Features 45 top requests of the martini crowd: Alfie • Beyond the Sea • Blue Velvet • Call Me Irresponsible • Copacabana • Danke Schoen • Feelings • The Girl from Ipanema • I Will Survive • Mandy • Misty • More • People • That's Life • more.

00310193 ....$14.95

Best of Cole Porter

38 of his classics, including: All of You • Anything Goes • Be a Clown • Don't Fence Me In • I Get a Kick Out of You • In the Still of the Night • Let's Do It (Let's Fall in Love) • Night and Day • You Do Something to Me • and many more.

00311577 ....$14.95

Big Band Favorites

A great collection of 70 of the best Swing Era songs, including: East of the Sun • Honeysuckle Rose • I Can't Get Started with You • I'll Be Seeing You • In the Mood • Let's Get Away from It All • Moonglow • Moonlight in Vermont • Opus One • Stompin' at the Savoy • Tuxedo Junction • more!

00310445 ....$16.95

The Best of Rodgers & Hammerstein

A capsule of 26 classics from this legendary duo. Songs include: Climb Ev'ry Mountain • Edelweiss • Getting to Know You • I'm Gonna Wash That Man Right Outta My Hair • My Favorite Things • Oklahoma • The Surrey with the Fringe on Top • You'll Never Walk Alone • and more.

00308210 ....$16.95

The Best Songs Ever – 5th Edition

Over 70 must-own classics, including: All I Ask of You • Body and Soul • Crazy • Fly Me to the Moon • Here's That Rainy Day • Imagine • Love Me Tender • Memory • Moonlight in Vermont • My Funny Valentine • People • Satin Doll • Save the Best for Last • Tears in Heaven • A Time for Us • The Way We Were • What a Wonderful World • When I Fall in Love • and more.

00359224 ....$22.95

Torch Songs

Sing your heart out with this collection of 59 sultry jazz and big band melancholy masterpieces, including: Angel Eyes • Cry Me a River • I Can't Get Started • I Got It Bad and That Ain't Good • I'm Glad There Is You • Lover Man (Oh, Where Can You Be?) • Misty • My Funny Valentine • Stormy Weather • and many more! 224 pages.

00490446 ....$17.95

FOR MORE INFORMATION, SEE YOUR LOCAL MUSIC DEALER,
OR WRITE TO:

HAL•LEONARD™ CORPORATION

7777 W. BLUEMOUND RD. P.O. BOX 13819 MILWAUKEE, WI 53213

0204

www.halleonard.com

Big Books of Music

Our "Big Books" feature big selections of popular titles under one cover, perfect for performing musicians, music aficionados or the serious hobbyist. All books are arranged for piano, voice, and guitar, and feature stay-open binding, so the books lie flat without breaking the spine.

BIG BOOK OF BALLADS
63 songs.
00310485 ....$19.95

BIG BOOK OF BIG BAND HITS
84 songs.
00310701 ....$19.95

BIG BOOK OF BROADWAY
70 songs.
00311658 ....$19.95

BIG BOOK OF CHILDREN'S SONGS
55 songs.
00359261 ....$14.95

GREAT BIG BOOK OF CHILDREN'S SONGS
76 songs.
00310002 ....$14.95

MIGHTY BIG BOOK OF CHILDREN'S SONGS
67 songs.
00310467 ....$14.95

REALLY BIG BOOK OF CHILDREN'S SONGS
63 songs.
00310372 ....$15.95

BIG BOOK OF CHILDREN'S MOVIE SONGS
66 songs.
00310731 ....$17.95

BIG BOOK OF CHRISTMAS SONGS
126 songs.
00311520 ....$19.95

BIG BOOK OF CLASSIC ROCK
77 songs.
00310801 ....$19.95

BIG BOOK OF CLASSICAL MUSIC
100 songs.
00310508 ....$19.95

BIG BOOK OF CONTEMPORARY CHRISTIAN FAVORITES
50 songs.
00310021 ....$19.95

BIG BOOK OF COUNTRY MUSIC
64 songs.
00310188 ....$19.95

BIG BOOK OF DISCO & FUNK
70 songs.
00310878 ....$19.95

BIG BOOK OF EARLY ROCK N' ROLL
99 songs.
00310398 ....$19.95

BIG BOOK OF GOLDEN OLDIES
73 songs.
00310756 ....$19.95

BIG BOOK OF GOSPEL SONGS
100 songs.
00310604 ....$19.95

BIG BOOK OF HYMNS
125 hymns.
00310510 ....$17.95

BIG BOOK OF IRISH SONGS
76 songs.
00310981 ....$16.95

BIG BOOK OF JAZZ
75 songs.
00311557 ....$19.95

BIG BOOK OF LATIN AMERICAN SONGS
89 songs.
00311562 ....$19.95

BIG BOOK OF LOVE SONGS
80 songs.
00310784 ....$19.95

BIG BOOK OF MOTOWN
84 songs.
00311061 ....$19.95

BIG BOOK OF MOVIE MUSIC
72 songs.
00311582 ....$19.95

BIG BOOK OF NOSTALGIA
158 songs.
00310004 ....$19.95

BIG BOOK OF RHYTHM & BLUES
67 songs.
00310169 ....$19.95

BIG BOOK OF ROCK
78 songs.
00311566 ....$19.95

BIG BOOK OF SOUL
71 songs.
00310771 ....$19.95

BIG BOOK OF STANDARDS
86 songs.
00311667 ....$19.95

BIG BOOK OF SWING
84 songs.
00310359 ....$19.95

BIG BOOK OF TORCH SONGS
75 songs.
00310561 ....$19.95

BIG BOOK OF TV THEME SONGS
78 songs.
00310504 ....$19.95

BIG BOOK OF WEDDING MUSIC
77 songs.
00311567 ....$19.95

Contemporary Classics
Your favorite songs for piano, voice and guitar.

The Definitive Rock 'n' Roll Collection
A classic collection of the best songs from the early rock 'n' roll years – 1955-1966. 97 songs, including: Barbara Ann • Chantilly Lace • Dream Lover • Duke of Earl • Earth Angel • Great Balls of Fire • Louie, Louie • Rock Around the Clock • Ruby Baby • Runaway • (Seven Little Girls) Sitting in the Back Seat • Stay • Surfin' U.S.A. • Wild Thing • Woolly Bully • and more.
00490195 ....$29.95

The Big Book of Rock
78 of rock's biggest hits, including: Addicted to Love • American Pie • Born to Be Wild • Cold As Ice • Dust in the Wind • Free Bird • Goodbye Yellow Brick Road • Groovin' • Hey Jude • I Love Rock 'N' Roll • Lay Down Sally • Layla • Livin' on a Prayer • Louie Louie • Maggie May • Me and Bobby McGee • Monday, Monday • Owner of a Lonely Heart • Shout • Walk This Way • We Didn't Start the Fire • You Really Got Me • and more.
00311566 ....$19.95

Big Book of Movie Music
Features 73 classic songs from 72 movies: Beauty and the Beast • Change the World • Eye of the Tiger • I Finally Found Someone • The John Dunbar Theme • Somewhere in Time • Stayin' Alive • Take My Breath Away • Unchained Melody • The Way You Look Tonight • You've Got a Friend in Me • Zorro's Theme • more.
00311582 ....$19.95

The Best Rock Songs Ever
70 of the best rock songs from yesterday and today, including: All Day and All of the Night • All Shook Up • Blue Suede Shoes • Born to Be Wild • Boys Are Back in Town • Every Breath You Take • Faith • Free Bird • Hey Jude • I Still Haven't Found What I'm Looking For • Livin' on a Prayer • Lola • Louie Louie • Maggie May • Money (She's) Some Kind of Wonderful • Takin' Care of Business • Walk This Way • We Didn't Start the Fire • We Got the Beat • Wild Thing • more!
00490424 ....$18.95

Contemporary Vocal Groups
This exciting new collection includes 35 huge hits by 18 of today's best vocal groups, including 98 Degrees, TLC, Destiny's Child, Savage Garden, Boyz II Men, Dixie Chicks, 'N Sync, and more! Songs include: Bills, Bills, Bills • Bug a Boo • Diggin' on You • The Hardest Thing • I'll Make Love to You • In the Still of the Nite (I'll Remember) • Ready to Run • Tearin' Up My Heart • Truly, Madly, Deeply • Waterfalls • Wide Open Spaces • and more.
00310605 ....$14.95

Motown Anthology
This songbook commemorates Motown's 40th Anniversary with 68 songs, background information on this famous record label, and lots of photos. Songs include: ABC • Baby Love • Ben • Dancing in the Street • Easy • For Once in My Life • My Girl • Shop Around • The Tracks of My Tears • War • What's Going On • You Can't Hurry Love • and many more.
00310367 ....$19.95

Best Contemporary Ballads
Includes 35 favorites: And So It Goes • Angel • Beautiful in My Eyes • Don't Know Much • Fields of Gold • Hero • I Will Remember You • Iris • My Heart Will Go On • Tears in Heaven • Valentine • You Were Meant for Me • You'll Be in My Heart • and more.
00310583 ....$16.95

Contemporary Hits
Contains 35 favorites by artists such as Sarah McLachlan, Whitney Houston, 'N Sync, Mariah Carey, Christina Aguilera, Celine Dion, and other top stars. Songs include: Adia • Building a Mystery • The Hardest Thing • I Believe in You and Me • I Drive Myself Crazy • I'll Be • Kiss Me • My Father's Eyes • Reflection • Smooth • Torn • and more!
00310589 ....$16.95

Jock Rock Hits
32 stadium-shaking favorites, including: Another One Bites the Dust • The Boys Are Back in Town • Freeze-Frame • Gonna Make You Sweat (Everybody Dance Now) • I Got You (I Feel Good) • Na Na Hey Hey Kiss Him Goodbye • Rock & Roll – Part II (The Hey Song) • Shout • Tequila • We Are the Champions • We Will Rock You • Whoomp! (There It Is) • Wild Thing • and more.
00310105 ....$14.95

Rock Ballads
31 sentimental favorites, including: All for Love • Bed of Roses • Dust in the Wind • Everybody Hurts • Right Here Waiting • Tears in Heaven • and more.
00311673 ....$14.95

FOR MORE INFORMATION, SEE YOUR LOCAL MUSIC DEALER,
OR WRITE TO:

HAL•LEONARD®
CORPORATION
7777 W. BLUEMOUND RD. P.O. BOX 13819 MILWAUKEE, WI 53213

Visit Hal Leonard Online at www.halleonard.com

Prices, contents & availability subject to change without notice.